The
Lifetime
LOVE AND SEX QUIZ BOOK

♥

The *Lifetime*®
LOVE
and
SEX
♥ ♥ ♥
Quiz Book

PEPPER SCHWARTZ, ♥ PH.D.

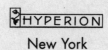

New York

A C K N O W L E D G M E N T S

I first started writing love and sex quizzes for a terrific but transitory dot-com called Sagestreet.com. I profited there from the talented editing of Allison Gardy. Later, I suggested continuing the quizzes for Paula Derrow, first my editor at *Glamour*, then again at Lifetimetv.com. I am in her debt for her friendship, guidance, fine editorial eye and encouragement to put these quizzes together in a book. Her successor, Holly Pevzner, has continued the chain of excellent editorial help and useful topic suggestions. This would not, however, have become a book were it not for the enthusiasm and support of my editors Mary Ellen O'Neill at Hyperion and Rick Haskins at Lifetime Television.

I really am blessed working with the intelligent and generous people who have been involved with this project. This includes a number of friends and colleagues with whom I endlessly discuss the conundrum of relationships. Many thanks to the following people who gave me great ideas for topics and questions (whether they knew it or not!): Jane Adams, Ginny Anderson, Cynthia Bayley, Julie Blacklow, Lisa Cohen, Laurie Beckleman, Martha Brockenbourough, Adam Berliant, Dominick Cappello, Ullrich Clement, Duane Dahl,

Ray and Gail DaMazo, David Deetz, Charlie Ebel, Cynthia Epstein, Linda Farris, John Gagnon, Paul Goldberger, Tina Gurvitch, Debra Haffner, Ruth Kraus, Janet Lever, Margaret Larson, Dave Kerly, Marty Klein, J. J. McKay, Sharon Nelson, Donna James, Toby Hiller Ziegler, Allison Harris, Bethany Hornthal, Karl Lutz, Nancy Mee, Susan Mercerieu, Linda Mitchell, Kate Pflaumer, Virginia Rutter, Linda Farris, Simone Reitano, Barbara Risman, Carol Schapira, Rick Schenkman, Maya Skolnik, Julie Speidel, Michael Schwartz, Herb Schwartz, Phil White, Phil Ziegler, and Gary and Angela Schwartz.

Finally, thanks to my family—Cooper, Ryder and Art Skolnik (and a special thank you to our housekeeper and sanity keeper Linda Cobb)—for tolerating the eccentricities that writers think of as normal (such as staying at the computer late into the evening, weekends and vacations) and for giving me their love and support.

C O N T E N T S

SECTION TWO
Everything you need to know about the right love for you and how to maintain love in a relationship

SECTION THREE
All about handling issues of possible conflict or momentous decisions

SECTION FOUR
What you need to know about building a great sex life

I N T R O D U C T I O N

These quizzes were written to give you deeper insight into pressing emotional and relationship issues, and to offer guidance in making important decisions. As a professor of sociology and a long-time researcher of love and sex, I have used my many years in the field of relationships to base these questions and answers on the best advice and information clinicians and researchers have discovered. Unlike a lot of the quizzes that are printed in various kinds of mass media, these quizzes are guided by psychological and sociological findings.

How should you interpret your test results? While each quiz is scored, I don't think the score is the only part of the quiz that's helpful. Some quizzes have explanations of what each question might tell you about yourself; I think that in these cases, you might get even more out of that analysis than an overall "grade" on the quiz. Sometimes the commentary is lighthearted, but the advice is serious. I hope these quizzes help you learn to be truthful with yourself.

Of course no quiz is meant to be equivalent to a therapist's analysis of your situation. If you are really worried about something, I'd suggest seeing a trusted counselor of some kind. Still, I think the process of answering the questions in this helpful guide will be more personally revealing than you might have imagined.

I would love to hear how taking these quizzes has affected you. If you have the urge, feel free to give me some feedback at Lifetimetv. com and/or join me there for chats on life, love and sexuality. And if you can think of any other subjects you would like a quiz on, let us know at Lifetime and I'll consider your idea for my online column.

Sincerely,
Pepper Schwartz, Ph.D.

Dating: What you
need to know about
yourself—or about
him—to find what
you're looking for—
and keep it

♥

Are You Ready
to Date Again?

♥

Whether it was a great love affair that fizzled, or a toxic relationship that finally went bust, the end of a relationship is downright traumatic (even when breaking up is the right thing to do). But venturing out into the dating pool again can feel even *more* traumatic, especially if it has been a few years (or decades) since you've sat through one of those awkward, endless first-date dinners. Not sure you're ready to dip your toes in? Answer these questions and find out.

Respond TRUE or FALSE.

1. The thought of seeing a romantic chick flick makes you want to spit.

2. You can now successfully listen to the theme song from *Titanic* without tearing up.

3. You can say with confidence that an evening at a romantic movie with your girlfriends will *not* result in a display of waterworks.

4. Lately, you've been primping, spritzing and styling. Frankly, you're into being noticed.

5. Flirting seems like too much work, or corny and uninteresting. Sexy gossip annoys you.

6. When you think of your onetime love, the rage still boils over.

7. You've sealed the "ex files." You haven't told a breakup story or sung "your" song in months.

8. When your thoughts turn to your old relationship, you secretly fantasize about being together again.

9. Those feelings of must-find-a-man desperation have dissipated.

10. You look in the mirror and think, *I'm smart, I'm attractive— I'm one desirable dame!*

SCORING

1.	TRUE = 0 points	FALSE = 1 point
2.	TRUE = 1 point	FALSE = 0 points
3.	TRUE = 1 point	FALSE = 0 points
4.	TRUE = 1 point	FALSE = 0 points
5.	TRUE = 0 points	FALSE = 1 point
6.	TRUE = 0 points	FALSE = 1 point
7.	TRUE = 1 point	FALSE = 0 points
8.	TRUE = 0 points	FALSE = 1 point
9.	TRUE = 1 point	FALSE = 0 points
10.	TRUE = 1 point	FALSE = 0 points

0–3 POINTS

You're still in recovery (for now). You're reeling over your breakup and your emotions are close to the surface. You need to be in a better frame of mind before you get out there again. Work hard to put the past behind you by spending time with people you care about before you bring someone new into your life.

4–6 POINTS

You're on the mend. Your heart is still pretty fragile, but there's light at the end of the tunnel. Focus on doing a little "head work" before putting yourself out there. Dating can be wonderful, but you have to be able to survive a few disappointments and even a couple of dating disasters. That means you need to feel good about yourself when looking for a new partner.

7–10 POINTS

You're ready and willing! You may find yourself getting a tad nostalgic, especially on holidays and Saturday nights, but you're over the worst of the breakup blues. The only barrier now? Plain old dating jitters. Get over them and get on with it!

11–13 POINTS

You're a dating goddess. All your senses are functioning nicely. You've put the past behind you (for the most part) and now you're just looking for someone who is good enough. You go, girl!

ANALYSIS

1–3.   Sad songs and sappy flicks only upset sad people. If Celine Dion gets you all worked up or a romantic movie brings on some serious tears, there's a good chance you're probably still raw and hurting. Once you're able to see (or listen to) a tearjerker without crying, you've cleared an emotional hurdle—and may be ready to date again.

4.   You're not ready to date if you're not ready to strut your stuff. And if you're really looking disheveled (or not bathing or changing your clothes regularly), you may be seriously depressed. See your doctor right away.

5.   If you're not into flirting—or even stories about flirting—there is something inside of you that needs to be turned on before you are ready to date. Once that glint has returned to your eyes and you find yourself being more playful with men (even men who aren't serious contenders), that's a good sign you're ready to get back into the game.

6.   If you were over him, you wouldn't feel so passionate. Not only is that no fun for you, it's probably no fun for those around you. Any perceptive guy will know that you are still too engaged with your ex to focus on the present.

7.   There's nothing less attractive (or more boring) than someone who shreds her past partner and goes on endlessly about what happened in that relationship during a date. If you can't let go of your fixation, stay at home until you get over it, or vent to your girlfriends. Otherwise, you might screw up some perfectly promising relationships before they even begin.

8.   If you're secretly—or not so secretly—hoping that your ex will come crawling back, you'll sabotage any date you have. If you don't put your last relationship to rest, you'll be dragging dead weight when you meet new people. That's not fair to them, and it's no fun for you, either.

9.   Never date when you're desperate! If you're miserable alone, jumping feverishly back into searching for The One will scare off just about every guy you date. If you feel too vulnerable and anxious, do group-singles stuff for a while or send e-mail to people, so that you can boost your confidence level before you actually meet a potential love interest in person.

10.   When you dive into the dating pool feeling good about yourself, you'll be more attractive to others, and will attract the people you deserve—those who feel good about themselves.

What's the Best
Kind of Dating for You?

You may not have realized it, but you have options about how you meet someone. This doesn't mean that you can get rid of all dating downers, but it does mean that dating can be more fulfilling if you pick a dating style that has your name on it. Take the following quiz, and it might give you some insight that will save you a few lumps in the short run as well as in attaining your larger goal.

1. **I am a party animal.**

    a. Describes me perfectly.
    b. Occasionally.
    c. I'd rather chew glass.

2. **If I see someone who appeals to me, I figure out a way to start a conversation.**

a. That's me.
b. I can do it, but not easily.
c. That is a bad joke.

3. **I like being fixed up on dates by friends.**

   a. It's a recipe for disaster.
   b. I think it can be awkward, but I have done it or would do it.
   c. If they have the same taste in people as I do, it would be my preference.

4. **I think a blind date is no big risk.**

   a. Sure, if it's bad, I can handle it.
   b. I would do it, but I hate the idea.
   c. I loathe the idea.

5. **The idea of writing letters back and forth to someone I've never met seems romantic.**

   a. Didn't they invent the telephone to fix that?
   b. Not my favorite, but I could do it.
   c. In another life I was a Brontë sister . . . this sounds like me!

6. **I think joining a hobby club—like a hiking, golf or museum group—to meet people is a good idea.**

   a. I can do that by myself.
   b. It's okay, but not my first choice.
   c. I'd like that; I'd have a better chance of meeting people I like.

7. **I think I can meet people who are good long-term material through my religious institution.**

a. That is the dead last place I would go.
b. I'm not too hopeful, but I would try it.
c. That's the first place I would try.

8. The idea of meeting someone in my profession or work-place appeals to me.

a. Way too close contact for comfort.
b. Sounds attractive—if it didn't complicate things too much.
c. This would be the best—I would know a lot about this person, and we would have something in common.

9. I like the idea of high-tech dating. Online picture personals, no problem!

a. I'm ready to sign up.
b. It intimidates me, but I would look at other people's ads—and then maybe try it.
c. Oh, sure. Expose myself to prying eyes? I don't think so.

10. Seatmates on planes, trains, and in other public places are date material.

a. Definitely. If I were attracted, I would be aggressively pursuing conversation.
b. If the other person started the conversation, and it was good, I would go for it.
c. I would not generally start a conversation; I certainly wouldn't give my phone number.

SCORING

Count up how many *a*'s, *b*'s and *c*'s you have. I'll give you an overall score on your dating profile, but see the analysis section that follows for more in-depth information.

4 OR MORE A'S

You are an adventurous dater. You don't like being hemmed in by conventions and you are willing to take a chance that might turn into a bad date if there is also the chance of being happily surprised. You depend a lot on instinct and chemistry—and you are willing to be the pursuer as well as the pursued. What you don't want to do is let someone else (friends, family, background) organize your social life for you. You probably have a pretty active social life, but you've also probably taken your lumps. Take a look at all these dating possibilities to see if maybe you've overlooked one that might not be your natural way of doing things, but could have some possibilities.

4 OR MORE B'S

You are not usually aggressive, but you are open to the suggestion of new possibilities. You are a mix of unconventional and traditional dating modes—and probably all you need is someone helping you get over your natural caution (like a friend who says, "Let's go to a party even though we don't know anyone there!"). You'll have a lot of varied dating opportunities. If you have quite a few *a*'s as well as *b*'s, you are a good mix of making opportunities happen and putting on the brakes when it looks unpromising. If most of your other scores are *c*'s, you need more romantic and familiar surroundings—which is fine, as long as you make sure you don't cut out too many dating options because they seem too crass.

4 OR MORE C'S

You are risk aversive and pretty traditional in your dating tastes. You are probably looking for someone very similar to you—and so you are looking in channels that are more known and comfortable. That might be the best way for you—but unfortunately sometimes those networks get used up—and you are no longer meeting any new people that way. You need a few more *a* responses or at least some *b*'s if you are going to up your chances of meeting someone. That doesn't mean you should be a "party animal"—but it might mean being a little friendlier to people you don't know—or go try out activities that are new. Look at some of what these dating styles are really like in my explanation of questions—you might find that you have skipped something that is really within your comfort zone.

ANALYSIS

1.   More people than you might guess are NOT party animals. Parties are stressful for most people—hence the amount of liquor they start taking in just as soon as possible. They are hard places to make a good connection—and if you love them, you probably thrive on the nervous energy and sexual vibes that big parties produce. That can be the beginning of a great night—less often, of a great relationship. Still, for those of you who shudder at the mere thought—don't completely write them off. Some parties are a good place to meet someone early on before people are too plastered. Remember there are parties—and then there are *parties*. You might find some of them more to your liking than others.

2.   Starting a conversation with a stranger is a great skill for daters. If you are a person who needs "chemistry" to be at all interested, then you'd better be good at fishing and hunting—which

means you go out and look for the animal rather than wait around, hoping it shows up in your backyard! If you responded with an *a*, you can go to places that need conversational "guts"—large parties, dances, bars—and you can take advantage of chance meetings in public spaces because you know how to get to know someone quickly. If, however, conversation doesn't come easily to you, these places are probably more torture than opportunity.

3.   If you like being fixed up, this means two things: Either your friends are similar enough to you that their taste in dates parallels your own (unlike, say, your parents' . . .) or you are open to a number of different kinds of people, and whatever they come up with is worth a shot. If you can do this, it opens up many more possibilities, because people often surprise themselves—happily as well as unhappily—if they take a chance. Another thought: If you *can't* imagine being fixed up by friends, maybe you need some friends who are more on your wavelength!

4.   If you answered *a*, you risk taker, you! This is even more adventurous than being fixed up. If you are ready to meet someone cold, it means you have courage and optimism (not to mention resilience, since some of these people are bound to be less than you hoped for). It bodes well for your being able to handle almost any dating situation.

5.   This is kind of a trick question; being a pen pal might seem romantic—and it *is*—but it also is quite conservative and practical. You want to really get to know someone before you meet them, yet you are brave enough to develop a relationship on paper with someone you get to know at a distance rather than up close and personal. This is a good dating style if you are a person who likes friendship as the basis for dating, and—surprise—it's no longer done mostly on paper. Online dating is a modern equivalent of 19th-century letter

writing. A person sees a picture or "chats" with someone they like online, and then they may e-mail and write for months and months before they actually decide to meet each other—and find a way to do it. This is a dating mode for people who want an in-depth, serious relationship with someone—and for romantics who have a practical side.

6.   People who like affinity groups don't generally like high-risk dating, blind dating, or dating that requires small talk. If you picked this kind of dating, you like something that at least gives you a good time, if not a serious partner. Of course that's a good thing too. You want less pressure, less risk—and an easy way of being with someone. You like it to be light before it gets heavy.

7.   You are probably a traditionalist if you chose this option. Sure, you may meet people other ways, but you are not looking for adventure. You want someone like you—with your values, your background, and your culture. You need to date close to home base. You know what you want and you are not too interested in negotiating differences on the major anchor points of your life. You would consider being fixed up by someone you knew who had similarly strong values and who would only think of a guy with the same goals and lifestyle as yours. Some online dating might be good if it was through religious channels (not necessarily because you are religious but because it would be a safer place to meet someone "nice").

8.   If you refuse to consider the workplace option, you are either the world's most disciplined person or you have the world's least desirable colleagues! Both traditional and risk-taking daters choose this mode—but the more cautious person knows it has a big downside: What happens when a date doesn't work out and you have to face each other—or work together? This is only a good dating style

for someone mature enough to resume the previous work relationship and hold no obvious hard feelings that interfere with the job.
Since this is harder to do than preach about, workplace romances
often lead to workplace exits. So before you decide to date in this
way, decide how much you love your present job.

9.   High-tech dating is good for both traditional and unconventional daters. Traditionalists can write an ad that specifies exactly
what kind of person they want (and can even go to specialty online
dating services, such as Jdate for Jewish people), and shy traditionalists can just look at other people's ads and never have to put one of
their own into the mix. Cyberspace is a good place for both serious
and ambivalent daters. Most people who use online dating are looking for that special someone; but for others the web is a good place to
get their feet wet after a long, dry period—like trying to date again
after a breakup, long illness, personal crisis, or divorce. While it
might seem to be a kind of environment that concentrates on looks,
there is a lot of evidence that it is only partially based on the pictures.
There is enough information for anyone who is looking for a soulmate to find one. It allows you to take your time—or meet quickly.

10.   Seatmate conversation is definitely not for the faint of heart.
It is a major move, because if they turn out to be not so great, there
you are, stuck with them for the next several hours whether you like
it or not. The meeting could turn into a quasi-date right there, but it
is not a tactic for the cautious. Still, the whole world is traveling these
days, and if you see someone great, it might be worth finding out if
he or she is available. A lot of people do meet on public transporta-
tion—and if conversation is one of your best features, you have the
time to make an impression on a seatmate.

Are You a Flirt?

♥

Are you shameless when it comes to making it clear that you're interested in someone—or would you rather die than give a "come hither" look (much less actually talk with or touch) to someone you don't know? Answer these questions and find out where you fall on the flirting scale.

Respond TRUE or FALSE.

1. You're chatting with the best-looking guy you've spied in months. When he's talking, you look directly into his baby blues—without once lowering your gaze.

2. There's nothing like the presence of an attractive man to get you cracking jokes and telling your funniest stories.

3. You've just been introduced to your best friend's cousin. As you chat, you find yourself smiling a lot more than usual.

4. It's 1 A.M. and you're still talking it up at the bar with a handsome man you met several hours earlier. Although you're

obsessing about how nice it would feel to touch (or be touched by) this guy, you keep your hands to yourself. You wouldn't dare give even a pat on the arm to someone you don't know.

5. You're not afraid of saying sexually suggestive things to get a reaction from someone whom you're attracted to. A little bit of titillating talk never hurt anyone.

6. You're not the type to "turn on the charm." If the conversation and laughter aren't flowing between you and a potential love interest, too bad.

7. When getting ready for a girls' night out (read: scoping for prospects), you like to wear clothes that show off the best aspects of your figure.

8. You're minding your own business, sipping your morning latte, when you notice a Brad Pitt lookalike checking you out. You instantly begin carrying yourself differently (not in a slouchy way, but in a hey-look-at-me way).

9. You've been known to let your leg brush against a fellow dinner guest's leg (if he's cute and available, that is).

10. Super-close dancing with an attractive stranger is simply not your thing. There will be no pressing of breasts, hips or butts while you're boogying on the dance floor, thank you.

11. Even when pressed, you steer clear of sharing stories about your passionate past.

12. You've been called a tease by more than one man.

SCORING

1.	TRUE = 1 point	FALSE = 0 points
2.	TRUE = 1 point	FALSE = 0 points
3.	TRUE = 1 point	FALSE = 0 points
4.	TRUE = 0 points	FALSE = 1 point
5.	TRUE = 1 point	FALSE = 0 points
6.	TRUE = 0 points	FALSE = 1 point
7.	TRUE = 1 point	FALSE = 0 points
8.	TRUE = 1 point	FALSE = 0 points
9.	TRUE = 1 point	FALSE = 0 points
10.	TRUE = 0 points	FALSE = 1 point
11.	TRUE = 0 points	FALSE = 1 point
12.	TRUE = 1 point	FALSE = 0 points

SCORING

0–3 POINTS

You're in a flirting famine! You're definitely not the flirting kind. That's okay, as long as you realize that there's nothing wrong with showing interest, or releasing a bit of sexual energy. Flirting doesn't make you "easy"; it simply makes you open to new people. A certain amount of back-and-forth banter can also get your blood pumping (not to mention everyone else's). So don't be afraid to flirt if you want to—just a bit. Think of it as your personal celebration of being a woman.

4–8 POINTS

You know how to flirt when you want to. You've mastered the art of giving off sexual energy without leading anyone on. Men feel flattered by your attention, and you feel more alive after a bout of flirtatious banter. Nothing wrong with that!

9–12 POINTS

You're a ferocious flirt. There may be times when you are in danger of crossing the line, flirting-wise. There's nothing wrong with showing romantic interest with a pointed glance, a soft touch or a toss of your hair, but if you're all over everybody (literally and figuratively) and you have no intention of getting involved sexually, you'll wind up creating frustration for everyone involved. Tone your "come hither" ways down a bit. You don't need to go overboard to get someone's attention.

Are You Inviting or Daunting to Men?

♥

Why are some women always meeting handsome strangers, while others can't even get a gent to stand next to them at a bar? There may be a systematic problem here. Let's see if we can find it!

Respond TRUE or FALSE.

1. When an attractive man walks into the room, you walk over and immediately start chatting him up.

2. When a man looks at you across a crowded room, you immediately beam back.

3. When you meet a man, you think the best thing is to be honest and open about your strong opinions.

4. If you meet a compelling guy under casual or business circumstances, you will only wait so long before calling him first.

5. If you meet a guy and you start an e-mail relationship, you find yourself e-mailing him quite often, even if he doesn't respond as often as you write.

6. You always immediately return his phone calls.

7. You have always been the one to say expressions of affection or love first.

8. You act sexy and available when you first meet a guy who attracts you. You ooze possibility.

9. On the dance floor you let it all hang out. Only a blind guy wouldn't notice you.

10. You try not to, but honestly, you tend to talk about old boyfriends and previous dating experiences when you are chatting up a guy you don't know that well.

SCORING

Give yourself one point for each TRUE response.

0 POINTS

Spending a lot of time alone, eh? Come on, look up! He won't think you're a hussy! Will yourself across that room and at least say something to Mr. Possibly Wonderful. Consider this a command, a sign from the cosmos. You need to become more sassy!

2–4 POINTS

You are friendly and forward, and you meet a lot of guys this way (but be careful: sometimes you may verge on the *too*-friendly category). Still, in general, men find you inviting and accessible. All those interested are likely to apply . . . and not worry about being bowled over.

5–7 POINTS

You are definitely bold. You let your feelings show, maybe a little too much, probably a little too early. Consider somewhat less personal exposure until you know the guy a little better. Let him work harder to get to know you. It's great that you go after what you want, but if you find yourself having short, rather than long, relationships, you might consider taking it slower so that you know if the relationship is worth having—and give the guy some time to want to know you more.

8–10 POINTS

Bet you know that you can be scary! Hurricane Force. Seriously consider backing off a little. You may be wonderful, beautiful, and have all kinds of intelligence, but a guy can only take so much of a good thing. If you responded TRUE to almost every statement on this quiz, you need to exercise more restraint during the early days of dating (and please lighten up about your old boyfriends—this is really a no-no. Save it for mutual confessions after you two are betrothed).

Do You Merit
a Second Date?

Dating 101 isn't offered in high school, which is why, when it comes to real-life romantic encounters, many of us end up feeling more like a dunce than the teacher's pet. To the rescue: our crash course in first-date etiquette. Answer these 14 questions, read our advice and start acing those rendezvous now!

Respond TRUE or FALSE.

1. You're just not one of those laughing, smiley types. Occasionally, people have even accused you of being too serious.

2. You don't really put *too* much thought into your first-date outfit. You prefer to come as you are. You've got a certain style and if your could-be-love-interest doesn't like it, tough.

3. Your favorite first-date activity is seeing a great movie.

4. When it comes to social engagements (including first dates), you find planning ahead to be *bo-ring!* You prefer not to be pinned down and don't like having to figure out what to do until the very last minute.

5. When you develop a crush, you have no problems letting your feelings be known.

6. You love to tell stories, particularly about silly things you've said and done in the past.

7. You know you shouldn't, but occasionally you'll reflect on past relationships during a first date.

8. You love to be a seductress on a first date, down to the double entendres, meaningful glances and initiating footsie under the table. But you generally know better than to have any serious sex.

9. You're not into traditional gender roles. Generally, you insist on splitting the check.

10. Meet a first date at a bar or restaurant? No way. You prefer to be picked up (or to pick up your date) at home.

11. Friends would generally describe your laugh as, well, loud.

12. To calm your nerves and help the conversation flow on a first date, you generally knock back more than a couple of glasses of wine.

13. You pride yourself on being an open book. The word *secret* is not in your vocabulary, even on date number one.

14. You make up your mind about people on the spot.

SCORING

Give yourself one point for each TRUE response.

0–5 POINTS

You're a first-date dynamo. Woo-hoo! Your first-date rating is very impressive. It's a good bet that you rarely go on just one date with someone if you're interested.

6–10 POINTS

You're a so-so courter. Your dating skills could use some fine-tuning. Keep reading for some insight.

11–14 POINTS

You're a first-date disaster. Dating doesn't come naturally to you for any number of reasons. Check out the advice below and set yourself up for a new debut.

ANALYSIS

1. You may be giving off a vibe that screams, "I'm a lot of work—and not very much fun." If you want to warm up a prospective main

squeeze, trade that somber demeanor for a ready smile. Being a serious person doesn't preclude having a sense of humor.

2.   Presenting yourself a bit more carefully doesn't necessarily mean that you're hiding your true nature. In fact, it's a good idea to think about who you might be instead of who you are—and that includes putting your best face forward.

3.   First dates are for getting to know each other, which is tough to do at the local multiplex. If you need a flick fix, make sure to include dinner afterward; that way, you'll have something to talk about over appetizers. Otherwise, your date may remember the plot of the film, but walk away with barely an impression of you.

4.   Most of us aren't flattered to be last-minute additions to someone else's weekend schedule. So plan ahead, and use the extra time to think about something you've been meaning to do for a while, say, snagging tickets to hear your favorite local band or going ice-skating at an outdoor rink. If you pick the right activity, your first date will be set apart from the usual dinner-and-drinks rendezvous.

5.   If you tell all too soon, your date may feel overwhelmed or—worse—think you spill your guts to everyone. Sharing gory personal details (e.g., a bankruptcy, a bad divorce, a traumatic childhood) is fine after you've spent some time together, but they'll sound like red flags if revealed prematurely.

6.   Too much self-deprecating humor isn't funny; on the contrary, it screams low self-esteem. No one, except maybe you, wants to hear endlessly about you, no matter how funny you are.

7. Do not reflect on past relationships on a first date! If revelations are necessary, make them as brief and as neutral as possible. You just don't know a first date well enough to (a) assume he's interested; (b) know if he will empathize with your ex more than with you; or (c) tell if he is imagining that some ex of his is talking about him in exactly these terms—and he's hating you for it. Consider this an unbreakable rule.

8. Flirting is good. Being seductive and then withdrawing is not. Sure, seductive behavior might keep your partner interested for a while, but eventually he's bound to get ticked off. If you act like a sexpot, be prepared to deliver in the not-too-distant future; otherwise, make your chaste intentions clear.

9. "Going Dutch" right off the bat can give a first date the feeling of a business partnership. A better idea: Whoever asks the person out pays for the first date, and the other person pays for the second.

10. From a safety perspective, it makes sense to meet at a neutral locale and get to know each other before anyone lays eyes on your abode. Plus, you may want to give it a little time before you start showing off your empty refrigerator, hyperactive dog or dust-ridden treadmill.

11. Does the volume of your laugh really matter? Yes. Loud laughter, a loud voice or making foghorn-like sounds are not turn-ons. A good rule of thumb when it comes to volume: If people you don't know turn to look at you when you laugh or tell a story, you're probably not being subtle enough.

12. Drinking and dating may seem synonymous to you, but it's never a good idea to get even a little drunk when you don't know

someone very well. Drinking dampens your inhibitions and makes it much more likely that you will commit all the dating mistakes mentioned above.

13.   Open books hold no mystery. It's better to be savored, chapter by chapter. Remain somewhat private—at least for a while.

14.   It's almost impossible to make a sound decision about someone on a first date. Sure, sometimes the chemistry is so lacking that you know immediately that you could never strike sparks, but usually it takes a while for people to unfold. Be open and remember not to rush to judgment.

Are You Unconsciously Looking for a Man to Be Your Dad (or the Dad You Never Had)?

♥

Sometimes we model our choices after dear old Dad in ways that we don't realize and that aren't necessarily realistic or good to look for in others. Take a look at this quiz, and see if you are a little closer to your dad than you think!

Respond TRUE or FALSE.

1. I find myself prioritizing characteristics in men that were the ones I liked most in my dad.

2. I find myself physically attracted to men who resemble my dad.

3.   I find myself attracted to men who have some of my dad's worst characteristics.

4.   I like men who are much older than me.

5.   I feel secure with men who remind me of my father.

6.   I like men who tell me what to do.

7.   I find that I get most involved with men whose approval I seek.

8.   I consciously compare the men in my life to my dad.

9.   When I was a kid I thought no one could measure up to my dad.

10. I find myself attracted to men who do the same kind of work my dad does/did.

SCORING

Give yourself one point for each TRUE response.

0–2 POINTS

Either you didn't have a very good relationship with your dad, or your choices run in the opposite direction by chance. You certainly aren't "Daddy's little girl" anymore, and you have almost completely independent tastes about what you want in a man.

3 – 5 POINTS

You probably had a very good relationship with your dad. It's nice to admire his qualities and want to find some of those in the man you love. You seem to have a good balance here; you want to replicate some things that you know are special, but you are not trying to look for someone who will parent you.

6 – 8 POINTS

Okay, we're getting a little obsessed here. Remember, you only knew your dad from a child's-eye view—not from a wife's. You are idealizing him a bit too much. Even if your dad was the greatest guy in the world, there are lots of different ways to be a great guy. Don't narrow your field so much.

9 – 10 POINTS

Uh-oh. How close is too close? This close. You are totally consumed in daddy worship—even to the point of being hooked on his flaws. You are, according to psychological terminology, "enmeshed," unable to differentiate yourself as an adult from your childhood self. . . . You need to grow up.

ANALYSIS

1. You like the same characteristics in other men that you liked in Dad? Why not? Just make sure you don't over-romanticize Dad and build him up (and his traits) in a way that is more idealistic than real.

2. No one attraction is more appropriate than another. Still, you might want to work on opening up your "love map" for a little more

geographical diversification. There really are a lot of ways for a man to be good-looking, and the one you have picked is fine—if it isn't the *only* way you think a man can be attractive.

3.   If you find yourself attracted to your dad's worst characteristics you have a problem. This is the kind of thing that leads women who had an alcoholic father to find someone who drinks. You don't have to repeat the past, even if it's what you know best.

4.   A lot of women like older men. They are usually more established in their careers, more experienced with life, and often kinder than younger men. However, if you find that you only like men *a lot* older than you, that might be a little too much homage to Daddy. Remember, if your husband is twenty years your senior, you may find yourself parenting him when he is older, just as he parented you when you were younger!

5.   Be careful about searching for security in any man. Especially if it's based on the fact that the guy reminds you of Daddy. Nobody can really provide an absolute guarantee of security. Marry a rich man, and he may lose his money. Marry a puppy dog of a guy, and he may still leave you for a bitch in heat. If you are looking for Daddy because you are really looking for security, you would do better to achieve for yourself, and marry (or stay in a relationship) for some other reason.

6.   You have developed a submissive personality: Be careful! This is almost guaranteed to attract someone who will ultimately treat you contemptuously. It may seem sexy in the beginning to be controlled by some manly guy. But after a while it will feel more like slavery. You don't want a man who likes control that much!

7.   For all of us who ever brought a report card home, worried that it wasn't good enough or waited for the judgment of a parent

about how we played in the game, there is a delicious similarity when we pick a partner who plays that role in our adult lives. The question is, Do you really want to bring home a report card for the rest of your life? That's no fun. Take on an adult-to-adult relationship instead.

8.   It's okay when you get serious about someone to think about whether or not they measure up to dear old Dad. But duplicating Dad is impossible, and having it as a conscious standard probably means you have over-idealized your father—and are undermining your relationship.

9–10.   Daddy worship is sweet at 6, silly at 36. Your dad might be (or have been) an extraordinary guy; but he is/was a human being. If you find yourself only considering lawyers as a mate because Daddy was a lawyer, you've gone too far. This is your *adult* life; let it play out the way it naturally unwinds instead of imposing your childhood script upon it.

Is He Your Friend . . . or Does He Want to Be More?

♥

You think you are buddies. But are there feelings lurking that might be something more?

Respond YES or NO.

1. Is he heterosexual? (If not, forget this quiz—and give up hoping that he wants more than friendship.)

2. Does he tell you about his dates, but not want to hear about yours?

3. Does he touch you a lot when you are together?

4. Does he act overprotective about you when you describe your present relationship?

5.   Does he act like he's the only one who knows you really, really well (and is your true soulmate . . .)?

6.   Does he always find something to criticize about your present lover?

7.   Does he joke about you and he getting together some day?

8.   Is his girlfriend/wife jealous of you?

9.   Has he asked you not to describe particularly sexual episodes?

10. Does he look sad when you say, "You're just like a brother to me" (or some similar asexual endearment)?

SCORING

Give yourself one point for each YES response.

0–3 POINTS

If there are only a few of these signs, they are probably just part of his affection for you. He really *is* being big brotherly—you can code him as a friend and be pretty sure that's really where he's at.

4–7 POINTS

The temperature is getting a bit too warm, a bit too possessive, a bit too "special." It might be time to face this head-on. Sure, it could be his respect and affection for you that makes him trash your boyfriend or tell you that your husband is not worth the floor you walk on, but I'm guessing it's more sexual than that. If you want him as a friend, make sure he knows it in no uncertain terms.

8–10 POINTS

This guy is just waiting for a sign, an opening. He dreams of you and is sticking pins in your sweetie's picture (ask your honey if he's had any strange aches and pains lately). If his significant other is glaring at you, then you know something is wrong. Time to set some clear boundaries—unless *you* are getting kind of misty-eyed thinking about *him* . . . in which case, time to talk.

ANALYSIS

1.   A lot of gay guys are flirtatious with women—they *know* it's never going to go further than that. What they forget is that you don't always have the ability to distinguish flirtation from seduction. If your friend is flirtatious, but you are not sure of his sexual preference—ask him! You need to know what is going on. If he's gay, you don't want to stress the friendship (and lose all those lovely compliments) by coming on to him. If it turns out he's not gay, it sounds like a great green light—if you want it to be.

2.   If he tells you about his dates, but doesn't want to hear about yours, chances are that he really is bothered by the idea of your being with other men. If you are interested in him, you might want to ask him straight out: "Why don't you ever want to talk about my relationships?" Maybe a light will go on in his head and he'll start asking himself the same thing!

3. If he can't keep his hands off of you, I'd call that affection, connection . . . and maybe even longing . . . Let your hands start to linger on him, see how he likes that! Let your eyes gaze a little longer . . . Start exploring sexy or romantic topics. This may be all he needs to know it is safe to pursue a romantic relationship with you.

4. Protectiveness could be friendship—or it could be jealousy. Whether he knows it or not, if he is vigilant about how you are treated and who takes up your time, that's a mark of attachment. Could just be friendship of course, but I'd say the more intense his protective feelings are for you, the more likely those feelings are more those of a lover than a buddy.

5. When you have a soulful connection with someone, you know it. And that can be true of either friends or lovers. So, this connection isn't one that readily lets you know whether he is a friend or would-be lover. But if he talks about it a lot and talks about how unique it is with you (and how lovely you are these days) you have to wonder, why couldn't it be part of a growing chemistry between you?

6. If he is always sure that no one is good enough for you—who do you think he thinks might be The One? Of course date trashing might just be the sign of an ungenerous nature, but if he's generally a good and supportive person, his continual downgrading of your romantic interests might be saying something.

7. Joking is usually a way of testing out possibilities without putting yourself at too much risk. It's easier to say "Can you imagine if you and I were setting up house together?" in a bantering way than to out and out declare himself to be fantasizing about a life together forever. Answer one of these jokes seriously. "Well," you might say, "that's not such a bad idea . . ." Then see what he does.

8.   There are few more telltale signs than if his lady looks at you with fear or distrust. If he is just your buddy, why should she be worried? Probably because he raves about you all the time! And if he does, she has every right to be worried. She may realize the truth: that he is smitten with you—whether he knows it or not.

9.   Most men love to hear about their friends' sexual encounters—unless they are jealous! If he isn't comfortable with swapping stories of sexual escapades, it might just be because he is a gentleman and he doesn't believe in such disclosures. But if it is only *your* sex life that offends him, I'd say it's because he wants you for himself.

10.   If he ever grimaces when you act like he's just a girlfriend, he may want to be something else. He may be looking for a cue from you indicating that you see him as a potential lover. If you are interested, try a seductive question or statement ("I bet you are a great lover," for example) and see if he takes the bait. He may no longer be cautious, trying to protect the friendship, if you give him an obvious opening to be something more to you.

Everything you need
to know about the
right love for you and
how to maintain love
in a relationship

♥

Rate Your Love I.Q.

What could be easier or more natural than falling in love? Than flirting and swooning and spooning? Than getting cozy between the sheets with the one you care about most? The truth is, sex *isn't* always instinctive, and the only easy thing about love is that too often, it feels easier to fall *out* of it than in. Still think you're a love expert? Answer these questions and see how heart-smart you are.

Respond TRUE or FALSE.

1. Going to bed mad is a big, fat no-no.

2. You can't *really* be in love if you still have strong feelings for a past flame.

3. When you meet The One, you will definitely know it.

4. Living together before tying the knot can only strengthen your bond.

5. Your ideal partner is someone very much like you, of course.

6. When choosing a life partner, it makes sense to go for a guy who has already sown his "wild oats."

7. If your partner still masturbates, it's a sign that something is lacking in your sex life.

8. Even if sex isn't mind-blowing at the beginning of a relationship, time (and practice) can eventually make it that way.

9. Jealousy in a partner is a sign of love and caring.

10. You should never have sex on the first date.

SCORING

Give yourself one point for each FALSE response.

0–4 POINTS

You need to stop accepting too much advice passed on to you by well-meaning relatives and friends! And you might even want to rethink some of your own approaches to relationships. Read the question-by-question analysis and see if there are some insights here that will change your mind!

5–7 POINTS

You've learned a lot in life, but you might want to read the individual answers to these questions to see if you have accepted some statements about love and sex at face value. They might not stand up on closer inspection.

8–10 POINTS

You have been schooled in the ways of love! You can tell a myth from a tip and you know that all of these statements overstate the case—or are downright wrong.

ANALYSIS

1. Numerous studies—not to mention your own experience—should tell you that solving problems when you're steaming mad is nearly impossible. Marriage researcher and therapist John Gottman, Ph.D., author of *The Seven Principles for Making Marriage Work*, has observed that when people get riled up, their heart rate and blood pressure rise and their emotions feel out of control—a phenomenon he calls "flooding." This hypersensitive state can last a good 25 to 30 minutes, during which you're not likely to be at your rational, problem-solving best. So hit the sack mad instead of continuing to bicker. You may toss and turn for a while, but you're likely to see things in a new light at dawn.

2. Forget everything written by Shakespeare. Human beings were meant to love more than one person during the course of a lifetime. Don't beat yourself up or conclude that you must be a bad partner just because you occasionally feel something for someone other than your mate. If your gaze strays, it just means that your juices are still percolating. (Acting on these feelings, on the other hand, is another story.)

3. We've all heard stories of Guy A spotting Girl B across a crowded room and, suddenly, breathlessly, just "knowing." What we *don't* hear are all those stories about people who "knew" and

were wrong. Besides, deciding on the spot that someone is your soulmate means you're less likely to be open to new information about that person. So don't act too soon—even if you are absolutely, positively certain that the cosmos was created just so you could meet this man!

4.   Nearly 50 percent of couples live together before marriage, but all that shacking up hasn't improved the divorce rate any. In fact, most research suggests that people who cohabit have a higher risk of splitting up than people who tie the knot first. While some experts attribute this disparity to the fact that couples with less traditional views are both more likely to live together and also to divorce, there's evidence that the experience of living together can change a relationship for the worse, making it less generous and committed than it might have been otherwise.

5.   Marriage experts have long held that sharing ethnicity, religion and other similarities is key to a lasting relationship. But reality suggests otherwise: Couples of different ethnicities don't have a higher divorce rate, nor do differences in age, hobbies or politics correlate with marital success or failure. What *is* important: shared goals and complementary personalities.

6.   If you want a partner who likes monogamy, would never betray you and is content to be with you and only you forever, then pick someone who never had any wild oats to sow in the first place! Research indicates that the best way to predict someone's future behavior is to look at their past behavior. So, while it's true that people can change, your best bet is someone whose personality and habits have been consistent. There really is a correlation, for example, between the amount of premarital sex someone has had and their likelihood of having extramarital sex. The more premarital sex, the greater the chance they will stray! Of course, *most* married people

are monogamous—still, if your guy has racked up extreme numbers of lovers, he has shown an unusual taste for adventure and variety. Unless his wild streak ended ten years ago, I'd be careful. Do whatever you like—but don't say you weren't warned!

7. If you crave a snack instead of dinner every now and then, does that mean you want to eat Oreos for the rest of your life? Masturbation is a quick and easy way to have an orgasm. Sometimes, your guy (or you) may want sexual release without emotional engagement, either because he's too tired, too distracted or too tense to commit to one-on-one sex. Masturbation also may correlate with a high level of horniness; people who masturbate a lot tend to like to have sex a lot. So don't interpret a bit of solo activity as a rejection—it's a sign that your mate likes sex and is willing to use a private moment for a quick hit of pleasure.

8. Sexual aptitude is like any other talent: Some people have it; some don't. Sure, those who aren't gifted between the sheets can learn to be adequate lovers, but if they haven't got a knack for knowing how to please you early on (and if they're not good at listening), chances are they never will. Plus, the beginning of a relationship is typically the most passionate, so if lovemaking is mediocre during those early months of infatuation, chances are it will stay that way. Sex therapy is very good at helping people conquer certain sexual issues, such as premature ejaculation or pain during intercourse, but it's much less successful in transforming those with low desire into lustful lovers. Sexual relationships do have a learning curve, and lovers who work at it can hit new heights, but a real mismatch is not likely to turn into sexual Nirvana.

9. It's easy to conclude that when a guy is possessively jealous it means he really wants you. But jealousy and possessiveness usually

stem from fear and low self-esteem, not love. Mature love is secure love. We know why someone would love us: We deserve it. Someone who's excessively jealous doesn't trust himself.

10.   Sleeping with someone too soon does not knock you out of contention for a "serious" relationship later, unless, of course, you're with a man who holds a double standard. Is that the kind of guy you want? We didn't think so. Sure, acting spontaneously and spending the night can bring you heartache if the phone doesn't ring the next day, but it can also create a connection. Risk-takers can lose big, but they can win big, too. (Just don't take risks when it comes to protecting yourself from *sexually transmitted diseases*.)

Do You Fall in Love Too Fast?

♥

You meet a guy: He's Russell Crowe handsome, smart without being snobby and laughs at all your jokes. Before that first date slides into good-night-kiss mode, will you: (a) find yourself sketching wedding invites on your cocktail napkin, or at least picturing how cute he'd look in his boxers; or (b) think that it might be nice to go out again—in a week or so? Answer the questions here to find out how fast you're likely to fall for your would-be dream guy.

Respond TRUE or FALSE.

1. After three fabulous dates, your current dreamboat whispers "I love you" in your ear during a hot and heavy moment. You find this proclamation highly suspect.

2. When you're in the throes of that giddy first stage of a new relationship, your window-shopping ritual inevitably turns from imagining fun stuff you'd buy for yourself to planning all the things you'd like him to buy for you.

3. After a handful of romantic rendezvous with a promising guy, you find yourself fantasizing about what your future children will look like.

4. In the past, you've fallen in love and quietly planned out in your own mind the future the two of you will share—even though you and the guy in question have never actually talked about anything further into the future than next week.

5. You don't want to jinx your newfound love connection, so you avoid mentioning your new main squeeze to gossip-starved friends and family until you have a sure sense of where things are going.

6. When you are head-over-heels infatuated, you're more likely to become a bit forgetful about birth control.

7. You've never dated anyone that you've actually believed could be The One.

8. You find yourself rationalizing situations that could be interpreted as warning signals. For example, he's often busy on Saturday nights, or he hedges when you ask for his home number, explaining that paging him, instead, would make it *so* much easier to stay in touch.

9. You love being in love. In fact, you've been in love more than five times in your life, not counting a few nights when you thought you were but he never called back.

10. In the past, you've fallen for men who, in retrospect, had completely different goals and values than you did.

SCORING

Use the following score key.

1.	TRUE = 0 points	FALSE = 1 point
2.	TRUE = 1 point	FALSE = 0 points
3.	TRUE = 1 point	FALSE = 0 points
4.	TRUE = 1 point	FALSE = 0 points
5.	TRUE = 0 points	FALSE = 1 point
6.	TRUE = 1 point	FALSE = 0 points
7.	TRUE = 0 points	FALSE = 1 point
8.	TRUE = 1 point	FALSE = 0 points
9.	TRUE = 1 point	FALSE = 0 points
10.	TRUE = 1 point	FALSE = 0 points

0–3 POINTS

You're a Realistic Romantic

Though you're not above making a few leaps of faith to explore a relationship's possibilities, in general, you're the type with your feet firmly planted on the ground. You feel your blood rush to all the right places when you meet a great guy, but you *don't* throw caution to the wind.

4–7 POINTS

You're a Daydream Believer

It's great to allow yourself those heady hormonal highs new love can bring, but be careful not to get too drunk on them. It's likely, with your susceptibility to falling in love, that you've already gotten a few blows to the heart and ego. And while there's nothing wrong with taking a few risks for love, you may want to be a bit more self-protective until those budding relationships have time to take root.

8–10 POINTS

You're a Risk-Taking Romantic

You are definitely in love with love . . . and you need to calm down! Sure, a couple of flings are worth the pain (the highs are so fabulous!). But by holding nothing back, you're bound to face more than a few disappointments. Look inside yourself and think about why you sometimes have difficulty allowing relationships to unfold. Are you hooked on the rush of new love, but less sure of yourself when it comes to conducting a real relationship? If so, you might need to work on building up your confidence and communication skills.

Is It Love . . . or Just Lust?

♥

We've all been drunk and dizzy with desire at the beginning of a promising romance. But what happens when those initially hard-hitting hormones subside and you're left with the sometimes-tough quandary: Is it *really* love? Answer these questions and find out.

1. **You've taken your partner home to meet your parents. And, surprise! Your family actually likes him—a lot. This makes you**

   a. Confused. If your parents love him, there must be something wrong with him.
   b. Relieved. You like him. They like him. No more harassment about finding a nice boy to settle down with.
   c. Feel threatened. Now your parents are *really* going to pressure you to make a commitment.

2. **You and your honey go on a magical trip to Paris. Beneath the Arc de Triomphe you have a big, fat argument, which leaves you both steaming. You**

a. Wonder if you're destined to break up.
b. Put your relationship on a slow burn for a couple of days, then, when you're tired of fighting, make up.
c. Feel mad for a while, then cool off.

3. **Between e-mails, coffee breaks and actual work, you find yourself daydreaming about your partner. Your thoughts tend toward**

a. What happened between the two of you last night, between the sheets.
b. Anxious fantasies about whether or not he'll be true to you.
c. The fabulous wedding you'll have—and how cute your future kids will be.

4. **You just bought yourself a great digital camera. As soon as you snap away, you realize your mate would go gaga over this technological wonder. You**

a. Plan on getting him one in the future, when the price goes down.
b. Offer to share your little gem with him.
c. Give him the one you bought. You know he'd use it more.

5. **You're at a dinner party with a roomful of people—some friends, some strangers—when your partner tells a joke that falls flat. You**

a. Turn a little red for him, the poor guy.
b. Laugh—loudly. You don't want him to be embarrassed.
c. Chuckle and remember again why you love his offbeat sense of humor, even if other people don't always get it.

6. **When you and your significant other are alone, you feel**

   a. The desire to entertain and interest him.
   b. The need to have sex.
   c. Peaceful, comfortable and intimate.

7. **Your partner has packed on the pounds lately. You**

   a. Don't think it matters. In fact, you're carrying a little extra something around the hips, too.
   b. Worry about his health, but you still find him erotic and lovable.
   c. Are completely turned off; you don't go for guys who aren't lean and mean.

8. **Your partner was offered his dream job in a city you consider to be in the middle of nowhere. He asks if you'd relocate with him. You**

   a. Say it's out of the question. You can't just up and leave your life for a mate.
   b. Say you'll consider it, but the thought keeps you up nights.
   c. Go. Home is where he is.

9. **It's your birthday and your main squeeze gives you a homemade card—complete with glitter and stickers. You**

   a. Smile, but your eyes dart around the room checking for your real gift.
   b. Smile, but are heartbroken that he hasn't bought you something.
   c. Smile. You're thrilled that he took time to make you something so sweet and from the heart.

10. **Your friend tells you that she saw your guy holding another woman's hand—and, no, he's not *that* close to his sister. You are**

   a. Not horribly concerned. There has to be a good reason and you'll ask when you see him.

   b. Furious. You drop whatever you are doing to ask what's going on.

   c. Crushed. You assume that he's about to leave you.

SCORING

1. a = 0 points	b = 1 point	c = 0 points
2. a = 0 points	b = 0 points	c = 1 point
3. a = 0 points	b = 0 points	c = 1 point
4. a = 0 points	b = 0 points	c = 1 point
5. a = 0 points	b = 1 point	c = 1 point
6. a = 0 points	b = 0 points	c = 1 point
7. a = 1 point	b = 1 point	c = 0 points
8. a = 0 points	b = 0 points	c = 1 point
9. a = 0 points	b = 0 points	c = 1 point
10. a = 1 point	b = 0 points	c = 0 points

0–3 POINTS

You're in a love-free zone. Either you're not in love, or you tend to love a bit cautiously (even a bit selfishly). Read on for tips on opening up your heart.

4 – 7 P O I N T S

Lust trumps love. You've got a lot of good things going, but this relationship may be mainly fueled by hormones—or even convenience. Read on to get a better sense of what's going on in your heart.

8 – 1 0 P O I N T S

You've got that lovin' feeling. You're madly—make that *intelligently*—in love! You and your partner are not just attracted to each other; you understand, accept and desire each other.

ANALYSIS

1. *b.* If you're really in love, you are happy if your partner connects to people who are important to you—you want him to get a sense of your past; and you like the idea that your parents are impressed by him.

2. *c.* If you're mature enough to sustain a deep relationship, you won't be crushed or ready to quit when you and your partner truly get into a big conflict. What matters is that you find a way to make up.

3. *c.* In the first stage of a relationship, your thoughts dwell on caresses, but when love is present, you start dreaming about a future.

4. *c.* Real love prompts generosity. The only thing better than getting something you want is giving it to someone you love. (Of course, if you are the kind of woman who starts thinking of a man as the father of your children while he's introducing himself I wouldn't give this question a whole lot of diagnostic weight!)

5.   *b*. You want to support someone you love. Or *c*: Because you love his offbeat sense of humor, even if other people don't always get it.

6.   *c*. If you're in lust, the first thing that occurs to you when the two of you are alone is to go at it. But when you're in love, you will often feel just as fulfilled being in each other's company.

7.   *a*. Ideally, your love is based on your partner's personality, not just the package these traits come wrapped in. If he has gained a lot of weight, *b* would also be a reasonable answer.

8.   *c*. Home is where he is. If you're in love, nothing should matter as much as being with the object of your affection. (Of course, if he loves you, he'll work equally hard to find a way for both of you to be happy.)

9.   *c*. You're thrilled that he took time to make you something so sweet and from the heart. If you really expect lavish tokens, maybe this relationship is not about him; maybe it's more about what he can provide for you.

10.   *a*. Not horribly concerned; there has to be a good reason and you'll ask when you see him. True love is secure and trusting. In most cases, if you feel in love—and loved—you are. If you are instantly jealous, it means that something is not right in the relationship.

Do You Value Love . . .
or Money?

♥

Okay—so you are supposed to value love in marriage above all other virtues or advantages. At least that's what Western culture says. But you know, a lot of cultures don't romanticize relationships—and certainly not marriage. In many countries marriage is arranged, because family ties and economic considerations are seen as the most important ingredients in a lifetime partnership. There is more than one way to think about what's important in life. So, I'm giving you permission to be honest here—and to find out what's really important to you. (If a question requires you to be married, and you are not, answer it according to what you think you would do if you were. If a question assumes you are single, and you are married, respond as if you were a single person today.)

1. **You are single and you meet a fabulously attractive person who wants to marry you. You are smitten—but not only will this person not make a lot of money, he/she comes with major debts. You**

a   Decide to marry anyhow.

b.   Decide you cannot afford to marry this person.

c.   Wait and hope he bails himself out of debt and the relationship holds together during this time.

2.   **You are in love with a person whose course of study requires an internship in the Northern Territories of British Columbia. You have been offered a high-paying job in Chicago and you think it is an extraordinary opportunity. Your loved one begs you to put it off for a year and stay together—in a place where there is no opportunity for you to do what you do best: make money. You**

a.   Put off your plans for a year.

b.   Break up. (How could he ask you to throw away such a great opportunity?!)

c.   Agree to e-mail and call as much as possible—and hope the relationship makes it.

3.   **You are in a serious relationship. Your partner can't afford it, but desperately wants to go to horticulture school to study the genetics of houseplants. It will be expensive, and there is no assurance that he or she will make a lot of money after graduation—in two to four years. You can afford to pay for this—but not without some suffering. You**

a.   Fork over the cash.

b.   Don't bring up the subject, because you'd have to refuse.

c.   Offer a partial formal loan with a payment plan.

4.   **Your spouse has gone through some tough financial times—his or her once bright career plans just haven't panned out. It has been three years since you've seen a paycheck that did more than cover a small portion of what you need to run a**

household. Since you have no children, your spouse has decided that there is some freedom to change careers and has plans to go into another line of work—work that is quite low paying. This isn't what you'd planned on. You

a.   Feel bad and seriously consider leaving.
b.   Feel bad, but you meant it when you said "for richer or for poorer."
c.   Try and make your spouse reconsider the new job choice—and make it clear that you want him to earn more.

5.   **Your partner is offered two jobs. One is his dream job, but the pay stinks. The other is an okay job, but he doesn't love it. And of course, the pay is sky high. You**

a.   Strongly pressure your partner to take the high-paying job—at least for a while.
b.   Tell him to follow his heart.
c.   Don't pressure your partner, but make it clear that you will be disappointed if he takes the low-paying job.

6.   **You are offered a job by someone your partner doesn't like (someone who has criticized his job performance in public). You know what he'd like you to say. But you really think this is a great opportunity and a lot of money. You**

a.   Take the job.
b.   Refuse the job.
c.   Try to convince your partner it is in both your interests—and if you fail to change his mind, you refuse the job.

7.   **You are engaged and meet the world's richest geezer. You wouldn't marry him just for his money—or would you? Mr. Mega-bucks understands your hesitation and says that if**

you will marry him and stay a devoted wife for ten years, you can walk away with five million bucks. Your present fiancé is, understandably enough, not supportive of this idea. You

a. Sign on the dotted line.
b. Refuse, because you wouldn't do this for money—even that much money.
c. Refuse, but only because of your fiancé. Otherwise, you might have done it.

8. **You have been invited by two men to go out on the same night. One you are in love with—he has invited you to his birthday party. The other is okay, but you don't want him—either emotionally or physically. He has invited you to the President's Inaugural Ball. It is not only an exciting prospect, but also could be very good for your business—you are a lobbyist. You**

a. Go to the birthday party.
b. Go shopping for a dress to wear to the ball.
c. Go to the ball, but only if the man you're in love with suggests it when he hears about the offer.

9. **You are about to be married. Two months before the wedding, your fiancé's whole financial world crashes. You were about to marry a CEO, and now the two of you can't even afford the wedding reception. Your intended is depressed and offers to let you cancel your wedding plans. You**

a. Are insulted. Of course this changes nothing.
b. Are relieved. Perhaps it shouldn't, but his financial woes change your feelings.

c. Are relieved. You hope that the economy will turn around and you can re-plan the wedding under better circumstances.

10. **Your lover has been in a bad accident. There are extensive facial scars. Plastic surgery would help, but it is very expensive—and your lover has no money saved for that. You do—but it would take all you have. You**

a. Immediately take it out of the bank.
b. Are emotionally supportive but contribute little or no money.
c. Contribute some—maybe have him sign a loan for a significant amount—but don't use up all your hard-earned cash.

SCORING

Give yourself three points for every *a* response, one point for every *b* response and two points for every *c* response. Look at your overall score, and then let's see what each response means.

0–12 POINTS

You have a heart, but it beats only when your partner's checkbook is healthy and your investments are doing well. You can't help it: Money is perhaps the single most important requirement of your life, and love comes in a distant second. No problem, but better make certain that your beloved knows the score.

13–17 POINTS

You like money more than you love love. You do love love, of course, but you are extremely pragmatic and you will not let your emotions—not even your emotional commitments—get in the way of your economic future. You might feel bad about it, but you think money is just as important as emotions—and you are not going to make financial sacrifices for the future—or even the present—just because of your heart.

18–24 POINTS

You value relationships over money, but you are a realist—and cautious about money. You aren't "selling out," but you know how important money can be, and you don't want to be parted from all of yours. You will make compromises, but you won't throw everything away in the cause of love.

25–30 POINTS

You are a romantic. You would sacrifice money for the one you love. You probably can't believe that anyone could do some of the things suggested in this questionnaire. Your whole life puts love in the center of what is important.

ANALYSIS

1.   Debts are a cost that quite a few lovers are not willing to bear. It's one thing to start out penniless, another to start out in the hole. A person with a super-romantic outlook would not care—but they might live to regret it. Someone who "loves more lightly" might be daunted by this—and might be right. The third choice is the pragmatic one: Let's see what this person can do when the chips are down. If the chips are always down, then maybe retreating from love isn't such an awful choice.

2.   This is an exaggeration of a choice that partners face all over the world. One person gets a great opportunity, and there is nothing there for the other. Can you love someone enough to give up your work (or home) for a year? Or (put the way a romantic would say it) do you love so little that you cannot donate one year out of your whole life for the good of your partner? This decision is the one that decides whether or not a lot of couples make it—or break up. Money is part of the decision—the rest is just how many of your own plans you will put aside, even for a finite time.

3.   How much are you willing to invest in your partner—literally? Sometimes a partner needs help, and the payoff is not huge, at least in dollars and cents. Sure, you hear about spouses putting their partners through medical school—they know that their lifestyle will benefit in the long run. But sometimes a partner wants an education that is not profitable but extremely important to them. It is a pure act of love to finance that endeavor for someone, because there is no fabulous payoff—just the knowledge that you have helped in making that person fulfilled. Would you do it? It says a lot if you would—or wouldn't.

4.   Sometimes you know something isn't temporary—it's permanent, and it means your partner's fortunes are not what you expected them to be. This is where the rubber, as they say, meets the road. Do you want to be with that person, or was it the combination of that person and the lifestyle you thought you would have together that makes the deal worth having? This is an awful situation if you realize it is the latter, because you know your love is not big enough to sustain the relationship.

5.   How much is your partner's happiness worth? Or, if you want to look at it another way—how much does your partner get to indulge

himself at the expense of everyone else? Depending on how you feel about money, one of these ways of looking at the issue will appeal to you more than the others. Do you feel that being able to love the job is more important than how much money you make? Or more to the point, no matter what you feel about yourself, how will you react if your partner's values are about self-fulfillment and not about economic success? Can your love survive if you feel the pay is too good to refuse—and your partner wants to refuse it?

6.   How would you feel if caring for his feelings would cost you a lot of money or a job you really liked? Would you refuse an offer if it came from someone your partner disliked? It's interesting to think about how much these feelings would count when money is in the equation.

7.   Be careful—this one might be hard to imagine, and therefore hard to be honest about. We are talking about five million dollars here, and if that doesn't mean a lot to you, why don't we up it to ten million? The question is, would you turn down a fortune if you really had this opportunity? If you don't even have to stop and think before responding, "There is no way . . ." then you are a dyed-in-the-wool romantic (or maybe just pragmatic if the reason you refuse is because you know you wouldn't be able to last long enough with this guy to collect the cash!).

8.   A birthday is an important celebration when you are in a love affair. But an inaugural invitation is a once-in-a-lifetime event—especially if it's a huge business opportunity. Would you chance damaging a blossoming relationship for a career move? Just how ambitious are you?

9.   Tammy Wynette tells us, "stand by your man," and that is what is expected. But if you stay, your choice will change the life you

thought you were going to have. Would you want the reprieve your fiancé has offered you—to wait until better times? What would you want to do, *even if you didn't feel you could do it*? Your answer shows you if money is integral to your ability to keep loving someone.

10.   The person you love has suffered a grievous injury. Helping will take everything you have. Could you do it? Your security is at stake, but your loved one needs you. A real romantic would see no other choice but to do all she could. A pragmatic person would do something but not put herself at risk . . . and a person who loved money more than love would be sympathetic—and keep that checkbook closed.

How Well-Matched Are Your Personalities?

♥

Have you had too many relationships that started out well and then self-destructed? Or are you wondering why you and your guy butt heads so often over what seem to be small things? It may be because the two of you have very different psychological profiles. Take this test and get a good sense of some important aspects of your own psychological profile . . . and how it fits with his! There is no overall scoring section here, just insight into which characteristics should be similar and which can be different.

1. **When I'm upset,**

   a.   I need to be by myself.
   b.   I seek the comfort of others.

2. **I am usually**

   a.   Optimistic about how things will turn out.
   b.   Cautious—it pays to look at the possible downsides first.

3. **I like**

   a. To stay flexible and not decide things until I have to. I don't mind changing my mind at the last minute.
   b. Closure—I tend to take in information, come to a decision, and act.

4. **I prefer**

   a. Spontaneity.
   b. Planning.

5. **When it comes to rules,**

   a. I like to break them when it makes sense to.
   b. I believe in honoring and following them.

6. **You could say that**

   a. My life is an open book.
   b. I prize my privacy. Life requires keeping things to oneself.

7. **I like to**

   a. Follow more than lead.
   b. Lead more than follow.

8. **When it comes to emotions,**

   a. I'm passionate and I've done some foolish things for love.
   b. I'm more cool than hot; I make my decisions about love very carefully.

9. **Taking risks**

   a. Makes me happy and excited.
   b. Scares me—I reduce risk as much as possible.

10. My energy level is

    a. High—I'm constantly on the go.
    b. More laid back; life shouldn't be frenetic.

ANALYSIS

1. Are you a People Person or Your Own Person? This question concerns your method of self-soothing. When your life is miserable or challenging, do you search inside yourself for strength and stay solitary until you find it? Or do you seek the guidance and comfort of a loved one or friend? A People Person needs others to help them heal. If you're Your Own Person, you and your partner need to know that this type is self-sufficient and reaches out to a partner only when things are under control. Try and tip toward similarity on this one. If your partner focuses inward and you look outward, you may be unhappy when you want to work as a team on problems.

2. Are you an Optimist or a Pessimist? Do you expect the best or the worst from life? Some personality difference is fine here. Optimists love other optimists—they need a sunny forecast. Occasionally, however, optimists are ridiculously optimistic—and they know it. So they seek someone who can provide a bit of balance. Pessimists really profit by having a partner who helps them open up and enjoy life. So, if you are the pessimist and always see the glass half empty, you would do well to seek an optimist to help you lighten up.

3. Are you flexible, or do you need closure? This question asks you how you make decisions. If you always like keeping your options open and can turn in another direction on a dime, you are flexible and probably take some pride in that ability. On the other hand, if you are driven to find solutions, you like to proceed in a log-

ical line of thought and action, get your information, reach a conclusion, and act. You'd better pick someone who is similar to you on this one. Otherwise, you will drive each other crazy! If you are a person who likes closure, your flexible partner will seem indecisive and flaky. If you are flexible, a partner who needs closure will seem anxious, unimaginative, rigid and maybe insecure.

4.   Are you a spontaneous person or a planner? If you are spontaneous, you are never too far away from your "inner child." You like to play—you like surprises and quirky, sudden possibilities. If you are a planner, however, you don't think that it is very responsible to wait until the last minute to decide what you are going to do. And it's too disappointing if things don't happen as they were supposed to! Most often, it's best to be similar. Sometimes, however, planners want to be more spontaneous, and so they attach to a freer spirit. If people are different on this one, they have to be careful to be sensitive to each other's need for closure—or lack of it!

5.   Are you a Rule Breaker or a Rule Follower? Rule Breakers can't resist breaking rules. Rule Followers find security in rules. They think that people who break them are childish—even dangerous. Better be similar on this one. People who care about rules really care about them. The Rule Follower feels that if no one obeyed the rules, the world would be totally chaotic. On the other hand, the Rule Breaker thinks that rules are oppressive and usually stupid. Does it sound like these two people should be together?

6.   Are you an Open Person or a Private Person? This question concerns your need for disclosing feelings and information (and expecting the same) or your preference for playing your cards close to your chest. If one of you shares and the other doesn't, one person will feel denied intimacy and the other person will feel pushed. The Open Person may be suspicious, feel unloved or worry that an affair

or some other terrible thing is going on. The Private Person may feel unsafe with the Open Person and will definitely not like being probed or prodded at home for his or her innermost thoughts. There is the possible exception of the Private Person who, over time, finds that he or she would like to be opened up. But don't count on that!

7.   Are you a Leader or a Follower—or a bit of both? This question is about control issues. Do you like to be in control of a situation, or would you rather have someone else call the shots? It's fine if one person shows a strong preference for being the Leader and the other for being a Follower. Watch out for similarity. If both people want to be the Leader all of the time, it can cause tiresome power struggles. It also doesn't work if you have two Followers, because both people are just longing for someone to take charge—and no one wants to!

8.   Are you Red Hot or Cautiously Cool? What is the essence of your romantic nature and your love style? Do you want to run on instinct and have a life that has unpredictable thrills and spills? Or do you make your love decisions slowly, carefully—always considering the long-term possibilities and consequences?

The cool person is not usually swept away by the passionate—and the passionate person seeks ways to win over the cool. Still, the initial attraction may not last for the long run. The cool person may revert to his or her essential nature, and the passionate person needs passion to stay interested.

9.   Are you a Risk Taker or Risk Avoider? This question asks how much of an edge life has to have to keep a person happy (or, conversely, how much of an edge a person can tolerate before they are unhappy). If one of you needs to live on the edge of a cliff and the other gets nauseated just looking over the side, you have a problem. In general, it's best if a person looks for someone who likes the same

level of adventure and has the same risk tolerance. Otherwise, the Risk Avoider will worry that the Risk Taker will undermine their life together and the Risk Taker will feel stifled and not respected.

10.   Are you High Energy or Laid-Back? How do you like to live your everyday life? The high-energy person needs to see a lot and accomplish even more to feel that the day has been well spent. The laid-back person wants to stop and smell the roses—or do one thing well and not keep going and going and going. In general, people should have similar energy. Otherwise one feels stifled and the other feels pulled, pushed and compromised in his or her quality of life. A *moderate* difference, however, can work to each person's advantage. The high-energy person slows down and doesn't burn out; the low-energy person gets roused to have a more varied and interesting life than he or she might otherwise.

Are the Two of You in Sync?

The habits and preferences you and your partner have may be out of sync. That's not necessarily bad. You might find it merely inconvenient—or even useful, because you compensate for each other. On the other hand, some habits that are out of sync can be a real serious threat to happiness. The question is, do you know which habits really need to be synchronized and which ones can remain charmingly different? First, let's take an inventory of what you have in common and what you don't. Then we'll see which qualities can cause the relationship problems—and give you some suggestions about what you might want to do about them.

Respond TRUE or FALSE.

1. One of us is almost always on time; the other person is barely on time or just plain late.

2. One of us likes to watch TV before going to sleep; the other person likes time to read.

3. One of us likes to get things off his/her chest as soon as they get home; the other person prefers to talk at a later time.

4. One of us is a night owl, the other is asleep by 10 P.M.; one loves early mornings, the other is uncivil before 10 A.M.

5. One comes to conclusions quickly; the other likes to examine all possibilities.

6. One likes to use every available minute for "something"; the other person needs a lot of "down time."

7. One of us likes sex in the morning; the other person hates it, or only endures it.

8. One of us likes late, leisurely dinners; the other person is hungry at six, ravenous by seven.

9. One of us likes to put off big trips and acquisitions, for financial security reasons; the other of us has a "live for today" philosophy.

10. One of us likes to plan; the other likes spontaneity.

SCORING

Give yourself one point for each TRUE response.

0–2 POINTS

You must have been matched in heaven. Either you picked each other *because* you shared the same rhythms or you have been really lucky. However it happened, you are in almost perfect synchronization, and it probably makes for a pretty wonderful home life. Congratulations!

3–5 POINTS

Not a bad score! You have some differences, but you are in sync on at least half of this list. If the ones you are not matched on trouble you, you might need to start addressing them. A few of these can be real deal breakers. Read on to see which ones . . .

6–10 POINTS

If you are mismatched on more than half of this list, it means that you are being irritated regularly by each other. If you are the world's most understanding person, you can probably weather these differences. But if you are not a saint, these differences can turn into big issues.

ANALYSIS

1. Being on time will not make or break a relationship, but it sure creates a lot of needless conflict. The person who is on time begins to feel that her time isn't seen as important, so the issue becomes more about love and consideration than about whether or not you both get to see the beginning of the movie. This is a situation that is good for many indignant retorts and maybe even a few "scenes." Why not fix it? Try meeting much earlier than you need to (for example, have a really early dinner before a play) so there is room for mistakes. Or, stop making dates where time is important and avoid the problem altogether.

2.   This is another timing issue that belongs in the "irritating but not fatal" category. Readers really hate the TV blaring while they settle in for what they consider a habit that is far superior to Jay Leno. TV people often resent being told to turn it off or down; it's the way they unwind for the day. The best answer is to have the TV (or another TV) in a separate room—or get headphones. Best of all is to take the TV out of the room, close the book and be in bed together as a couple, and use this time for talking about your day or being affectionate or sexual with each other.

3.   This is the first serious issue on the list. The reason is that *when* you bring up things makes a big difference both to the person who is talking and to the person who is expected to listen. Having something on their minds really weighs heavily upon some people. The longer they keep it, the bigger it gets. If it doesn't get handled, resentment builds. The opposite style is when partners don't want to be bombarded with the issues of the day as soon as they walk through the door. They don't see life as an emergency and they don't like drama. If their partners insist on having an issue aired immediately, they feel cornered and pushed. They think of their partners as "high maintenance"—maybe even selfish. This timing issue can have serious consequences if couples don't forge a compromise.

4.   It isn't great when one person is asleep while the other person wants to talk or make love. Each person feels the other is inconsiderate—or avoiding him or her. Unless partners learn how to modify their sleep schedule, they will totally miss really important time together. Fortunately, this is easily adjusted. The person who likes to stay up late can come to bed early, talk or make love, and then stay awake after his or her partner goes comatose. Or, the partner who can't stay up can make a brave effort every now and then (e.g., mul-

tiple cups of coffee) just so the other partner knows he or she is try-ing. The same kind of tinkering can even smooth over one person's penchant for getting up at dawn and the other's for sleeping in. It can be annoying if the early bird wants the more sluggish partner to go out and get worms with him. If each partner in a couple can learn to operate more independently of the other, then this lack of sync is not so big a problem. However, not everyone can, or wants to try to, have this much independent bedtime behavior in their relationship.

5.   Another more serious synchronization problem. One per-son's habit of deliberation can drive a partner crazy if he or she needs closure and action—even if the other person hasn't had a chance to seriously consider the problem. Women, generally more than men, want to discuss feelings, and may or may not be ready for resolution. Men tend to want to come up with an answer—and move on. This can cause arguments between men and women when a woman just wants to vent and a man comes up with all kinds of action plans—and is puzzled when his partner says, "Can't you just listen!" This is not a trivial difference, and it takes some understand-ing and respect for the other person's style, because it probably isn't going to change.

6.   This difference needs management. One of you is the Ener-gizer Bunny; the other is a two-toed sloth. One of you loves the calm and ease of a lazy day with a good book. The other one sees every hour missed doing something as a wasted one. This difference in the way you enjoy life, timing and energy has broken up many an other-wise good relationship. It is a basic personality characteristic and hard to change, but it can be modified. The couple has to work out how to put together a good mix of alone time and couple time so that most of the time, each person gets to live at the pace he or she likes best.

7. In the beginning, couples want each other all the time. But when the excitement of the early days is over, they discover that their sexual desire happens at different times. This can become a real problem if each person is *never* interested at the same time as the other. But usually, unless some other issue is at work, partners can find some time when they both feel amorous. Partners who are particularly gracious can have sex for their partner's sake at a time that doesn't usually suit them (say, 3 A.M.). But no one should be having sex when it really turns them off.

8. This difference may cause the end of having the whole family at dinner, but still, it is relatively manageable. Some people have to eat when they are hungry. They literally can't wait or they get cranky or downright nasty. Others aren't hungry until later in the night—at 6 P.M. they are hardly interested in food. Some accommodations are necessary: sitting down together at six but actually eating at different times or breaking the family up into early and late eaters. It's a drag, but it's no big deal.

9. This is a big one. Some people feel life isn't fun unless you live it to the fullest *now*. Others want to plan for the long haul, live well within their means and save far more than they need to save. The "here and now" person thinks this is stupid, and might even feel that holding back is a comment on his or her ability to earn enough money. The partner who wants to wait, however, may feel that their security is being undermined by overspending. If the more cautious person's fears become true, she may not want to stay in a relationship that she feels puts her security at risk. Likewise, if she is the more devil-may-care partner, she may feel she is missing too much of life by saving and waiting. A solution: Each partner needs to live a little on the other person's terms—some spending, some saving, some impulsiveness and some caution.

10.   Some partners feel that fun only happens when it happens spontaneously. He doesn't want to know what will happen on the weekend until the weekend. He doesn't want to script a vacation; he wants to let it unfold. She, on the other hand, wants to know where they are going way ahead of time, so they don't miss anything. When he refuses to plan, it makes her really angry. When she nags him to plan, he thinks she takes the fun out of it. The answer: some planning, some spontaneity (and accepting the fact that it's not the end of the world if something cool is missed).

Is Your Relationship Commitment-Ready?

♥

Almost everyone in a serious relationship has come to a point when he or she has had to decide if this was the time to go steady, move in together or get married. When you get to that moment, you might start going down a personal checklist, trying to decide if this is the person and if this is the time. I'd like to help you with that process, so let's see if your relationship is commitment-ready.

1. **You are in a room of really attractive, successful people. You**

    a. Flirt, and imagine being with this or that person.
    b. Flirt, but don't really get interested in anyone.
    c. Feel lonely and miss your guy.

2. **Your partner has gained some unattractive weight. You**

    a. Are less attracted, and begin to worry if you are right for each other.

b. Are still attracted, but are upset and don't know what to say.

c. Figure out a way to foster healthy eating habits and exercise.

3. You meet your partner's family. You don't like them. You

a. Shrug it off—no big deal.

b. Get really worried and say how you feel.

c. Are not completely honest about how you feel but try to find out how your partner sees them and how they would participate in your life together.

4. You are offered a great job in another city. You

a. Know you are going to take it, no matter what.

b. Know you will take it—and hope to convince your partner to come.

c. Plan to talk to your partner before you seriously consider it.

5. Your partner has an annoying habit. You

a. Add it to the list of things you don't like and worry about it.

b. Figure it is just part of the cost of any relationship.

c. Talk about it and see if your partner is willing to modify it.

6. You and your partner

a. Own nothing together.

b. Own one or two things together.

c. Are not sure who owns what on a number of things—and don't care.

7. You have taken trips together and

a. It was hard—a lot of tough experiences.

b. It was fun, but you disagreed on plans or had different habits.

c.   Had a few differences but mostly you were totally compatible.

8.   On the topic of communication, you

a.   Can't think of many subjects you've discussed in depth.
b.   Have shared feelings or concerns about most, but not all, important subjects.
c.   Have shared feelings, argued and solved problems about sex, past relationships, work, personal values and family. There is nothing important you have not discussed deeply.

9.   Your sex life is

a.   Pretty tame now.
b.   Still exciting but you have some issues.
c.   Really good! You've worked it out.

10.   Your jealousy level is

a.   High. There are lots of times you feel you can't trust your partner.
b.   Medium. Occasionally you worry.
c.   Low. You feel very secure.

SCORING

Give yourself one point for each *a* response, two points for each *b* response and three points for each *c* response.

10–16 POINTS

You aren't ready. The two of you haven't learned how to discuss problems and how to work things out yet. In addition, there are plenty of things you're not sure you like about this relationship. Let's face it; you are ambivalent. When things aren't right, you doubt your choice—and you may not be too secure of your partner's commitment either. There is too much that isn't worked out here.

17–23 POINTS

Most of your house is in order, but to get this score you had to hedge on quite a few issues. You are afraid to take on some of the hard things that you need to address. You may not be ready to make sacrifices for the relationship—and most relationships require them sooner or later.

24–30 POINTS

The higher your score, the more secure and mature this relationship is. You are definitely not still looking, you have good communication and you balance protecting your partner's feelings with airing problems that need to be solved. You deserve to feel ready to devote yourself to this relationship.

ANALYSIS

1. If you have a roving eye at this stage in your relationship, something is wrong. Flirting is fun, but when you are in the throes of trying to see if this person is The One, it's odd behavior. If you realize

that you still need the oohs and ahs of someone new at a cocktail party, you should take that in as important information; it's telling you that your heart isn't signed, sealed and delivered. You are not ready to be committed.

2.   If minor changes in your partner's physical appearance really put a dent in your attachment, you obviously aren't deeply in love. On the other hand, if the changes are major and you don't let your partner know how you feel, he may ultimately change appearance so much that it hurts your sex life. You can communicate, however, when you both know you are committed to each other forever and everything is within a context of love and for the benefit of your relationship.

3.   If you are in a serious relationship, the parents are important for two big reasons. One, if you stay together, like it or not, they will be in your life; and two, a lot of times the apple really doesn't fall too far from the tree. Do those parents tell you anything you really need to consider about your guy? In any case, a commitment requires thinking about his parents as future in-laws. Bad or good, they will be in your life.

4.   It's not that true love demands living in one town—sometimes people have to separate for a while for work or school. But if it would never cross your mind to change your plans because of your relationship, then maybe you don't really think this is the love of your life.

5.   Annoying habits are not trivial. Small, icky habits might seem sort of eccentric when you are madly in love, but after ten years they might just drive you crazy. Committed relationships require some honesty so that small things can be handled before they become big

things. If you haven't dealt with the little things you dislike about each other yet, it means you aren't ready to be committed.

6.   People who want to be attached to each other create common things—like owning a chair, a dog or a house. If you are very careful not to owe each other anything or to keep fiercely independent, that's one way of keeping the door wide open. It's not that you have to pool everything—far from it. But the fact that you haven't intertwined anything probably means something.

7.   Traveling is a good test of a relationship. Travelers have to make dozens of joint decisions on any given day, and there are bound to be some times when each person wants to go in an opposite direction. The question is—do you have good compromise skills? If there is a lot of conflict—or if it all seems a lot more work than fun—then it doesn't look like you're a couple who has your act together enough to make a commitment.

8.   Two people who are trying to be a couple usually test the relationship by talking about their most personal goals, values and experiences. They want to test the water and see if it is deep or shallow. They take risks about controversial subjects or facts of their past. If something is holding one or both partners back, it could also be that one or both of you aren't ready to invest in the relationship.

9.   When you are really in love you think that commitment will solve issues like one person having a big sexual appetite and the other an itty-bitty one—or that love will heal sexual scars from wretched past experiences. But people who make a commitment knowing that sex is bad or absent or blah live to regret it. This area needs positive resolution before a stable commitment can take place.

10. If you are jealous because your partner is intentionally putting out signs that he is available, then he is a jerk, and you should leave. But if his mere presence near a woman makes you jealous, then you have to get rid of those feelings before you are ready for commitment. Jealousy is quicksand for a relationship—you simply can't build on it.

Do You Put Your Relationship First?

———— ♥ ————

Would you make plans with your best friend for Saturday night without calling your significant other first? Does the thought of taking a vacation without your main squeeze sound like not much of a vacation at all? Answer these 10 questions to see if your relationship is at the top of your to-do list or if you're a loner at heart—whether or not you're part of a couple.

1. **Your live-in love is due to return from a weeklong business trip at 2 A.M. You**

   a. Arrive at the airport, meet him at the gate and whisk him home to bed.

   b. Make sure he has reserved a car service to take him home (you tucked a few phone numbers in his suitcase), though you still feel guilty about not offering to come get him yourself.

   c. Don't even *think* about making the middle-of-the-night trek to the airport.

2. **Your partner is on a quest to shed a few pounds, and he's trying a faddish diet that requires he eat only specific strange foods. You**

   a. Learn how to whip up his special menus and jump on the diet bandwagon yourself.

   b. Help him get his new diet off the ground by sharing the grocery shopping and cooking, but you stick with your usual fare at dinnertime (or chat with him about why many current diet programs are unhealthy and try to convince him to eat healthy foods with you).

   c. Wish him luck, though secretly you're skeptical about how he'll manage in the kitchen. After all, *you* don't have time to prepare his meals.

3. **Your honey has been moaning about his aching back all week. You**

   a. Give him full-out massages for four or five nights straight.

   b. Give him two or three short but substantial rubdowns.

   c. Slip him the phone number of the great masseuse your sister raves about.

4. **Without your knowledge, your husband has offered the guest room to his incredibly annoying, highly critical Aunt Millie for the week. You**

   a. Smile and say you'd expect no less. After all, she is his flesh and blood.

   b. Agree to the visit, but calmly let your partner know you're miffed that he didn't check with you first. (Inside, you feel the urge to stomp your feet and slam the door. You can't stand that old biddy!)

c. Demand that he rescind the invite. After all, Aunt Millie is an evil old lady who upsets you every time she opens her mouth.

5. **Your mate leaves dirty dishes, week-old clothes and various other paraphernalia scattered around the house. You**

a. Make it a habit to clean up after him. He's not going to change and you're not about to live in Pigpen's dream home because of it.
b. Pick up the truly rodent-attracting items but leave less-gross things where they are and remind him that his stuff is *his* responsibility.
c. Leave the garbage exactly where you find it and tell him, repeatedly, to clean it up—or else.

6. **You and your love are trading sexual fantasies to act out when he springs one on you that, quite frankly, you find shocking. You**

a. Indulge him anyway. If you don't, he may go elsewhere for his fun.
b. Agree to give it a go, but just this once.
c. Refuse immediately. You would never humiliate yourself for a man.

7. **Your steady has taken a strong dislike to one of your closest friends. He's asked you not to invite her over anymore, and in fact, he'd prefer if you stopped being friends altogether. You**

a. Respect his wishes and slowly sever all ties.
b. Stop meeting your pal at your house but continue to see her elsewhere.
c. Tell him he has no right to ask such a thing, and continue seeing your friend whenever and wherever you want.

8. **Your husband is gung ho about investing in a funky fusion restaurant downtown, but he wants the money to come from your children's college fund. Your reaction:**

   a. After thinking long and hard, you agree to loosen the purse strings.

   b. You agree that you can allot some cash for this investment, but not all of it.

   c. You remind him the money is off-limits, except for the kids' education.

9. **Lately, your guy has been socializing with "friends" after work, though he has been vague about where he's been. You**

   a. Don't question him. After all, you don't want to upset him.

   b. Ask him what he's been doing, and feel better when he tells you who he's seen and where he's been.

   c. Demand accountability and check his alibi.

10. **Your partner has been known to raise his voice and say nasty things in the heat of an argument. You**

    a. Understand that he gets easily agitated, so you try to smooth things over until his mood has improved.

    b. Ask him to stop shouting and gently insist that he wait until he's calmer to express his feelings.

    c. Tell him he has no right to speak to you like that, and he should leave the house until he's ready to interact like a mature adult.

SCORING

Give yourself one point for every *a* response, two points for each *b* response and three points for each *c* response.

10–14 POINTS

You're a do-anything dame. The good news: You're a very loving person. The bad news: You're prime doormat material. If you continue to let your love walk all over you, you may lose your self-respect (and probably his respect too). It's fine to want to do things for the person you love, but that doesn't mean you have to act like a servant. Use your own judgment and resist pressure to do things you think are wrong. Most important, make an effort to take care of your partner a little less and yourself a little more.

15–20 POINTS

You stand by your man—and stand up for yourself. You may feel at times that you give in to your partner's wishes a bit more than you'd like to, but generally you're able to pull back and say no when something doesn't sit well with you. Feel good about your loving, giving qualities, but continue to stand your ground when necessary.

21–30 POINTS

You look out for number one—you! You definitely know when not to be a doormat, but sometimes you show a certain lack of kindness, which could undermine the health of your bond. Ask yourself whether you are still in love with your partner. If you aren't, do something about it besides being ungenerous. On the other hand, if you *are* still in love, ask yourself why you're having difficulty giving, and whether there's something your partner is doing that's making you angry. Doing some exploration could go a long way toward bringing you closer together.

Is There Enough Romance in Your Relationship?

♥

We chalk it up to the inevitable—romance is bound to fade after years of diapers, joint checking accounts and roof repair. Still, there's a reason that millions of people are mysteriously drawn to Meg Ryan flicks. Truth be told, most of us crave romance, but a lot of us don't realize how little we're getting. Answer these questions about yourself—and then, about your honey—and find out who is most responsible for making your relationship romantic—or romance starved!

All About You

Respond TRUE or FALSE.

In the past three months you have:

1. Made your mate his favorite dish (to awaken other appetites . . .).

2. Put on an outfit that you knew your guy would find irresistible.

3. Picked up a great bottle of wine or champagne and downed it—together.

4. Treated your guy to a candlelit rubdown (before he suggested it).

5. Slipped a note to your honey telling him why he still gives you butterflies (birthday cards don't count).

6. Went out on a real date, complete with dinner, drinks and hand-holding over the table.

7. Reminisced about some special moment in your relationship (such as your first date or the moment you both first *knew*).

8. Invaded your mate's shower or bath to wash his hair, scrub his back and lather up his body.

9. Awakened him in the middle of the night—or super early—to make love.

10. Lingered at the dinner table for a catching-up talk or walked the dog with him just to hear about his day.

11. Kissed him, spontaneously, in public.

12. Held his hand while watching TV, linked arms while crossing the street or put your head on his shoulder.

13. Touched his face tenderly.

All About Him

In the past six months he has:

1. Bought you a non-kitchen-related gift out of the blue.

2. Given you a massage just to make you feel good. (No return rubdown required.)

3. Noticed something you did to yourself (those subtle highlights) and complimented you.

4. Remembered an important date in your life, with no prompting.

5. Played social director for a wonderful just-the-two-of-you evening out.

6. Confessed to one of your nearest and dearest how much he adores you.

7. Sent you an e-mail or gave you a call just to tell you he was thinking about you.

8. Made foreplay a priority.

9. Treated you to a romantic weekend getaway.

10. Sat through a chick flick because he knew you'd like it.

11. Fed you from his plate in a sweet or seductive way. (Bonus points for in-bed nibbling.)

12. Told you how happy/grateful/lucky he was to have you.

13. Given you one of those weak-in-the-knees gazes.

SCORING

Score each section separately, giving one point for each TRUE answer.

YOUR SCORE

0–4 POINTS

Isn't It *Un*romantic
Either you're so busy you haven't noticed that romance has dropped off the radar screen, or you're teed off at your partner. Time to get talking—and get some sweet gestures going or you two risk a falling out you won't recover from.

5–9 POINTS

Lukewarm Lovers
You probably rationalize that your occasional romantic gestures are enough, but you're wrong. Even if you think that holding hands is corny and a morning shower is for cleaning, not canoodling, all relationships need sweetly intimate touches. So give more and you shall receive.

10–13 POINTS

Bitten by the Love Bug
You tell him you love him. You show him you love him. And you're always trying to do the things he'll appreciate, even if they're not always your cup of tea. A good mix of sexuality, caretaking and

exciting experiences are sure to make him feel that your relationship is as satisfying as it ever was. Congratulations. You get an A in romance.

HIS SCORE

0–4 POINTS

Courting Catastrophe
Help your hardheaded guy understand that you need more than just his carcass around the house. He must have been doing the romance dance when he was trying to win your affection, so try to get back in that groove. Wax nostalgic—without whining—about your early days as a couple and tell him how much you'd like to do some of the things that made you feel so right for each other in the first place. If he resists, there may be a serious problem that needs attention in the relationship.

5–9 POINTS

Not *Sooo* Bad
Your guy's got the idea: He tries to remember important occasions and makes a good effort to do things that make you feel wanted and understood. He may, however, think that what you call "the little things" (flowers, romantic dinners) are way over the top. It's up to you to teach him that they're not. A little effort, and you could get bumped into the super-romantic category.

10–13 POINTS

The Ruler of Romance
A guy with this big a heart should be deemed a national treasure! You're obviously on your man's brain, but don't take that for granted. Being adored is a gift, so be sure to reciprocate.

Is Your Relationship
Affair-Proof?

♥

Let's face it: It's pretty hard *not* to be tempted. Handsome strangers, sexy delivery men, charming business associates—affair possibilities are everywhere. So what is it that makes some stay monogamous and others make motel reservations?

Basically, successful relationships are like a tripod: They require *romance* to nurture and create passion and intimacy, *sexuality* to make each of you feel alive and uniquely bonded to each other and *communication* to know each other well and trust each other enough to find out what's really going on inside each of your heads. Neglect any one of these factors and your relationship may be at risk. Treat each part of the tripod equally well, and you should definitely be enough for each other forever. To find out if you and your partner have what it takes in all three of these areas, answer the questions on the next page.

Respond TRUE or FALSE.

1. Kissing between you and your partner is great. You do it when you leave each other in the morning. You do it at the end of the day. You kiss a lot.

2. You may not be as hot and heavy as you were when you first met, but you still have sex at least once a week. And you've been known to pull a few new between-the-sheets tricks out of your bag to keep the passion pumping.

3. You are *so* past that stage where you fuss over your face and worry about your wardrobe to try to look good for your partner.

4. You've packed on roughly 15 pounds since you and your honey have been together. Come to think of it, so has he.

5. At least one sexy little lingerie number has been introduced into your undies drawer this year.

6. Candlelit dinners, picnics on the beach, midnight swims—all these are distant memories. Worse, you haven't been on an honest-to-goodness date in months.

7. Occasionally, you two like to do the outdoorsy thing together: playing sports, driving in the country, yard-sale shopping or just taking a stroll.

8. Just-the-two-of-you time is a must. You go on a romantic weekend getaway at least once every three months.

9. Whether it's Deweyville, Utah, or the heart of Manhattan, when business trips arise, you both try to bring the other along.

10. Gift giving (and receiving) is limited to special days only, such as Christmas, birthdays and anniversaries.

11. You talk about your future—your dreams, goals and all that good stuff—at least once a month.

12. You think personal problems should be kept in the family. Neither of you would seek the help of a counselor, therapist or religious advisor, no matter what.

13. You and your partner are in constant contact. You touch base via phone or e-mail throughout the day. In fact, you always know how to reach each other.

14. You love to keep each other laughing (and each of you knows just what to say to get the other giggling).

15. Your man comes home from work and spills most of the details of his day. You do the same.

SCORING

Use the following score key.

1.	TRUE = 1 point	FALSE = 0 points
2.	TRUE = 1 point	FALSE = 0 points
3.	FALSE = 1 point	TRUE = 0 points
4.	FALSE = 1 point	TRUE = 0 points
5.	TRUE = 1 point	FALSE = 0 points
6.	FALSE = 1 point	TRUE = 0 points
7.	TRUE = 1 point	FALSE = 0 points
8.	TRUE = 1 point	FALSE = 0 points

9.	TRUE = 1 point	FALSE = 0 points
10.	FALSE = 1 point	TRUE = 0 points
11.	TRUE = 1 point	FALSE = 0 points
12.	FALSE = 1 point	TRUE = 0 points
13.	TRUE = 1 point	FALSE = 0 points
14.	TRUE = 1 point	FALSE = 0 points
15.	TRUE = 1 point	FALSE = 0 points

ANALYSIS

Questions 1–5.   You need at least four points here to have a relationship with enough heat in it to be affair-proof. If sex and seductiveness have been put on the back-burner, one or both of you could be longing for passion.

Questions 6–10.   If you have less than three points here it means that your relationship is romance deprived. You've gotten efficient rather than intimate. You may still have chemistry, but if you no longer have romance, one or both of you will feel distant—and even unloved. Take more time together, and get in touch with each other's feelings.

Questions 11–15.   If you have less than three points here you are in danger of losing your status as best friends. Communication isn't optional in a relationship: It's the most important way you know you are unique in each other's life. You may have drifted away from those long talks you had about hopes and dreams in the beginning of your relationship but it's not too late to bring them back. You need to be in each other's daily life—and be able to seek help if there is relationship gridlock.

Is Your Relationship
in a Rut?

♥

Sometimes your relationship is in so much of a rut, you don't even notice it. But we'll help you see if the classic signs of stagnation are in place. That's the first step to doing something about it!

Respond TRUE or FALSE.

1. You haven't had dinner in a new place in six months.

2. You haven't been out with a couple you don't know well in more than a year.

3. You haven't tried a new sport in a couple of years.

4. You haven't spent a morning just making love in a year.

5. You haven't gone on an adventurous vacation in a couple of years.

6. You haven't worn something new and glamorous for a night out in six months.

7. You haven't surprised your husband with a weekend away or a surprise party in two years.

8. You haven't tried a new hobby or revisited a favorite activity or spot the two of you used to like for a year.

9. You can't remember when your partner last said or did something that surprised you.

10. You haven't had occasion to miss your partner in at least a year.

SCORING

Give yourself one point for each TRUE response.

0–3 POINTS

You are in pretty damn good shape. You don't let too much time go by without injecting some new experience into your relationship—or taking care to nurture and preserve the things that sustain you as a couple. Congratulations.

4–7 POINTS

Watch out. While you are taking care to do a few new things, you are missing out on a lot of the things that used to give your relationship energy and sex appeal. Don't forget to keep doing things that make your partner fun to be around; don't forget to keep wooing each other every so often.

8–10 POINTS

A rut can become pretty deep pretty fast—time to climb out of it! You need to spend some time planning outings and new experiences. You might be quite satisfied with a lot of what you do together, but every relationship needs refreshing. Get serious about putting a little zest back in yours.

Are You Being Strung Along?

You're in a relationship that you want to turn into something serious: namely, marriage. But it has been going on and on without turning that crucial corner. Let's find out if this relationship is going anywhere.

Respond TRUE or FALSE.

1. Your partner has never bought you an expensive item as a gift.

2. Your partner has never fantasized with you about the future.

3. Your partner has never said "I love you" without your prompt (or outside of the bedroom).

4. Your partner takes more than an occasional short vacation alone.

5. When your partner takes a vacation alone it is sometimes not possible for you to get in voice contact—or know exactly where your partner is.

6. Your partner does not cover his fair share of the expenses.

7. Your partner has not met—or does not want to meet—your family and close friends.

8. Your partner has not introduced you to—or spent a lot of time with you in the company of—his family or close friends.

9. Your partner is making major investments without including and consulting you.

10. You do not, in your heart of hearts, feel this relationship is rock solid.

11. You could not just pop in on your partner without being worried about his reaction—or that you might find something embarrassing.

12. Your partner gets mad or defensive when you bring up the future.

13. Your partner is very reassuring when you feel insecure, but will never make definite plans for anything more committed than you presently have.

14. Your partner will not commit to any specific dates for getting engaged or married.

15. Your partner still acts seductive with other people.

SCORING

Give yourself one point for each FALSE response.

0–6 POINTS

This isn't bad if you are in a young relationship, but if you have been together for more than a couple of years, then I'd say there are flashing danger signs. Partners who have been together awhile should be pooling items, mixing with each other's family and friends—and should feel secure and trusting. You seem like you are still walking on eggshells and your lives are hardly joined together. If you are looking for a committed relationship, you may be wasting your time here.

7–11 POINTS

This relationship could be shaky. This score shows that there are a lot of things that should involve both of you but don't. Your partner is not making enough noises about a future and you are not putting enough things together that are indications of a serious commitment. You might just be early in the commitment process—but keep reading to find out about why these different steps are important—and keep a close watch on your progress.

12–15 POINTS

Good news: You seem to be in a real relationship. Your partner doesn't seem skittish and has integrated you into his life. A perfect score of 15 would be best of all, but even 12 is reassuring. I don't think there is any reason to worry.

ANALYSIS

1.   It may sound crass, but people usually give an expensive gift or two when they are madly in love—or planning a life together. Perhaps he displays his intentions in other ways that you find meaningful, but aren't expensive—writing a poem or a love song, for example. If you have never gotten a "serious gift" (or it's been a long time since he got you one) it may be a danger signal.

2.   People in love fantasize about the future. It doesn't *guarantee* a future to imagine what life could be like together ten or twenty years from now, but the absence of any such hopeful plans is a bad sign. If you start talking about future plans and your partner changes the subject, you're getting a message you should listen to—even if you don't want to.

3.   Saying "I love you" is important. If your partner has never said it, that's serious. If he used to say it and doesn't now, that's even more serious. Prompts by you don't count—it has to come up spontaneously. And *when* it's said matters too—if he says it only during sex, it's not worth much.

4.   People in love don't want to use their rare vacation time without their loved ones, unless there are some extenuating circumstances. Even then, I'd be worried if it happens more than once in a great while. If you are the person he is organizing his life around, he should also be organizing his free time to be with you.

5.   Your partner should always want you to be able to find him. Aren't you two a team? Wouldn't he want you to know where he is if you had any trouble in your life? If he's talking about how he needs his "space" or privacy, I'd be thinking, "For what?" He can have independence without having an unlisted number, turned-off cell phone,

or no hotel room number. If you can't find him, probably somebody else has.

6.   Generosity and fairness are important in a relationship. If your partner is planning to be with you, he should want to share expenses and help you out as much as he can. After all, aren't you heading into the future together? If he doesn't, it's a bad sign.

7.   Red alert! This is an important cue. Someone who is serious wants to know all about you—and also wants to impress your family and friends. He wants them to support his relationship with you. Unless you are estranged from your family—and there is some reason he can't meet your friends—a lack of integration here is bad news.

8.   Ditto on *his* friends and family. He should want to show you off and have all his friends tell him how lucky he is. Unless his family are all ax murderers and have killed off all his friends, you should know most or all of the people who matter to him. If he is close to his family and you aren't, this relationship isn't going anywhere.

9.   Some people keep their finances separate—so separate investing doesn't necessarily mean that much. But the majority of committed people think of their financial lives as intertwined. If your partner never discusses this part of his life with you, this could be a cue that you are not included in his future plans.

10.   Listen to your gut instincts. If you feel another person might come along and lure him away—or that he is still shopping around—there is probably good reason for your fears. If you have answered a majority of these questions as true, your fears are probably not unfounded.

11.   Partners in a good, long-term relationship should be able to take each other somewhat for granted. There should be respect for each other's plans of course, but you should be able to assume that your presence is welcome. If you feel insecure about your reception, something is wrong.

12.   Another red alert! Thinking about and talking about the future should be exciting and enhancing to a relationship—not an intrusion on the present. If you get defensive and angry reactions, your partner is feeling ambivalent, pressured or dissatisfied. Any of these bodes ill.

13.   Are you or are you not progressing as a couple? Protestations of love are not enough. New mileposts have to be established. A big vacation with a couple of close friends? A trip home to meet his parents? Make sure reassurances aren't empty promises. Something concrete should be happening.

14.   If you and he have been saying "I love you" for a long time now, and if you and he have been making declarations of commitment, somewhere along the way it's time to set a date. Or at least to set a date to set a date. If a couple of years have gone by, you should be able to set a wedding date or know the reason why you haven't— and agree with it.

15.   If your guy is still pouring it on when he is around attractive women, it doesn't sound like he is off the market! A little charm is okay, but seductive behavior isn't. He should act like there is only one important woman in his life—and other women should know it. If they seem encouraged to pursue him, this relationship may be teetering rather than gaining traction.

All about handling
issues of possible
conflict or
momentous decisions

♥

Who Really Has the Power
in Your Relationship?

♥

You're the bill payer, but he's the big moneymaker. You're a beauty queen while he's Joe Average. You've always been faithful and he's cheated. So who's got the power? Answer these questions to find out who *really* holds the cards in your twosome.

1. When it comes to the cold, hard stuff (money), who earns more—you or your partner?

    a.   I do.
    b.   My partner does.
    c.   We are on equal financial footing.

2. What's the gap, if any, between your respective bank accounts?

    a.   I have at least 30 percent more money than my partner does.
    b.   My partner has at least 30 percent more money than I do.
    c.   Both of us are equally in the money.

3. **When the two of you are having an argument (or simply chatting), who is more likely to interrupt?**

   a. I am.
   b. My partner is.
   c. We tend to interrupt (or not) equally.

4. **Who holds the veto power in your home, as in which movie to rent or what kind of car to buy?**

   a. I have no qualms saying, "That's *not* going to happen!"
   b. My mate tends to play the "That's *not* going to happen!" card more than I do.
   c. We both have equal authority to say, "No way!"

5. **Do you love your partner more, or does more love flow in your direction?**

   a. I love my partner more.
   b. My partner loves me more.
   c. The love flows equally.

6. **When it comes time to clean the closets, scrub the toilet or whip up dinner, who's most likely to get down to business?**

   a. I am pretty much the housekeeper and chef; my mate is not exactly domestic.
   b. In a pinch, my mate will help around the house, but he still ends up doing a lot less than I do.
   c. We aim to split the housework equally, more or less.

7. **Which one of you is happier with his or her career?**

   a. Most of the time, I feel pretty good about my work.
   b. Most of the time, my partner is beaming and chatting up a

storm about his exciting workday while I'm grousing about mine.

c.   Both of us are equally content (or miserable) with our work.

8.   Which one of you has more friends or outside interests?

a.   I have more independent relationships and interests than my partner does.

b.   My partner is definitely the social one.

c.   We both have a healthy share of friends and outside interests.

9.   Has either of you cheated?

a.   I'm the one who has strayed.

b.   My partner has had an affair, but I haven't.

c.   Neither of us has cheated.

10.   Which one of you is more attractive to the opposite sex?

a.   I'm the half of the couple that attracts the most admiring glances.

b.   My partner is the looker.

c.   We're both equally attractive.

11.   If you and your partner were to break up tomorrow, who would suffer more?

a.   My mate would be riddled with heartache.

b.   I would be more devastated.

c.   Both of us would suffer equally.

12.   Who do *you* think holds the power in your relationship?

a.   I think I do.

b. I think my partner is the power hog.

c. Both of us are equally powerful.

SCORING

Give yourself one point for each *a* response, two points for each *b* response and three points for each *c* response.

0–21 POINTS

You've Got the Power

Whether it's your bulging bank account or your ability to dominate a conversation, you have the upper hand in your relationship. Possessing that power could make you happy, or it could make you long for a bit more balance. Many women (maybe even most) become uneasy when they call too many of the shots; if you know you can steamroll right over your honey, you're less likely to think he's sexy. How to redress that sense of balance? Watch your retorts (they may be a tad too sharp), and be careful not to always go your own way without consulting your mate. Use your power wisely and make sure your partner gets to shine too.

22–30 POINTS

Your Partner Has the Power

Initially, you may have been attracted to your mate's powerful qualities, but these same attributes can end up breeding resentment. You need to stick up for yourself a bit more. Couples don't necessarily have to be equal in every aspect of life (although the closer they get to that sense of equality, the happier they tend to be), but mutual respect and support are essential. Try focusing on an area where you sense an imbalance (monthly bill paying, for instance) and see if there's room for change. Trying to create a few small changes can go a long way toward making your relationship feel fairer—and happier.

31–36 POINTS

You're Equals

Congratulations! You two are a well-balanced pair. Though your partner may have more power in certain areas, overall, you both have clout—either because you work hard to divide things equally or because reaching equilibrium comes naturally. Like most power-balanced couples, you're probably pretty happy about the way your relationship works. More power to you both!

ANALYSIS

1–2. Studies suggest that money is a good predictor of power in a relationship, but it's not always the deciding factor. When men hold the purse strings, women are more likely to have to ask for household and personal money, which can put a damper on their independence. But when women earn more, men aren't necessarily second tier. That's because women tend to be more sensitive and aware of egos when they're the ones bringing home more bacon.

3. Research shows that if one person consistently and successfully can interrupt the other person, the one who interrupts is the more powerful partner.

4. In a truly democratic relationship, both partners are entitled to say no once in a while; when a relationship is unbalanced, one person predominantly exercises that right (which probably causes feelings of resentment in the other person).

5.   The best-loved partner usually knows it, and may take advantage by distancing himself or herself from the relationship. The one who gives more love usually has more to lose—financially and emotionally. The healthiest relationship is one in which both people feel equally lucky to have the other.

6.   In a truly equal partnership, both mates split chores pretty evenly, but when kids come along, women usually end up doing the lion's share of the parenting. But if the woman has an equally (or more) demanding job than the man does and still takes care of most—if not all—of the housework, she's the less powerful partner.

7.   Besides the obvious benefits conferred by a regular paycheck, having a fulfilling job increases self-esteem and gives each partner something to feel good about apart from their relationship. A person with a satisfying, well-paying job is also in a better position to leave the relationship, if need be, which enhances power.

8.   Having an extensive network of friends is a great self-confidence booster, and well-connected partners know that they have other people to turn to in times of trouble. And that's powerful.

9.   Having an affair may be a way of showing you have enough power not to worry about losing your partner if you get caught, but when a betrayed or neglected spouse goes out to "even the score," it also can be a way of equalizing power.

10.   Modesty aside, most of us are aware of our own "market value," partly because we have some sense of how others react to us. In general, a devastatingly beautiful woman (or a Tom Cruise look-alike) can choose from among more life partners than someone who is only average-looking can—and those options confer power. (In a

man's case, a few extra million in the bank can make up for one or two deficits in the looks department.)

11.   Often, when one person is more invested in the relationship than the other, a severe power imbalance results. The more that both partners are intertwined socially, emotionally and financially, the harder it is for either to leave, and the greater the incentive to work to stay together.

12.   Perception is everything. If you think someone has more power than you do, you probably cave in sooner, which of course makes your perception a reality. (The exception: If both partners feel that the other is more powerful, you'll end up with an unexpectedly egalitarian arrangement!)

How Do the Two of You Manage Stress? Do You Pull Together—or Apart?

———— ♥ ————

Sometimes the only way you know what a relationship is made of is when circumstances make it hard for you—or your partner—to be your "best self." Let's take a look at a few conditions and see how you behave when you are really pressed hard. Your score can be a good indicator of what might be a better way to handle certain stressors.

1. **You've planned a great trip for your anniversary, but a crisis at work makes it impossible for him to go. You are most likely to**

   a. Tell him that he always puts his work before the relationship.

   b. Pout, but understand there was nothing that could be done about it.

c. Plan a smaller celebration close to home, and figure out how to reschedule the trip.

2. You have been watching news of a tragedy; your partner indicates he would like to make love. You

a. Give him a look that tells him you think his behavior is utterly inappropriate.
b. Cuddle but don't make any move to make love.
c. Talk about what you are both feeling—then decide if you want to make love or not.

3. Your partner comes home and slams the door. He's obviously had a bad day. You

a. Glare at him and/or avoid him.
b. Get angry and tell him not to take this out on you. You ask him what is going on!
c. You don't get mad; you ask him if he wants to talk about it.

4. Your partner is supposed to be someplace he is not. You

a. Immediately get upset and worried and imagine he is hurt or with another woman or something like that.
b. Worry, but don't jump to extreme conclusions. You start trying to track him down.
c. You figure there is some non-traumatic reason and wait (for a reasonable amount of time) for him to call.

5. You realize that you owe more on your taxes than you have. When the two of you talk about it

a. One or each of you blames the other.
b. One or the other of you is near panic. One of you suggests major lifestyle overhauls.

c.   You take the time to figure out how you got there and what it will take to correct it in the future.

6.   You have a friend who is extremely ill, perhaps dying. You

a.   Don't share it with your partner. It is your friend, your grief. He probably wouldn't understand anyhow.

b.   Mention it abruptly and hit him with the full force of your sadness.

c.   Have let him in on this sad fact of your life from the beginning (ideally), so he knows what is going on and what it means to you. If it is sudden news, you let him know so he can comfort you.

7.   You receive a speeding ticket for reckless driving. You

a.   Deal with it yourself; you are embarrassed and don't want your partner to know.

b.   Deal with it yourself because you know your partner will over- or under-react.

c.   Regardless of how you think your partner will react, you share this information, because you need to think about this with him and decide what it means and how to deal with it.

8.   When the relationship itself feels rocky, you

a.   Say all the awful things on your mind.

b.   Don't get abusive, but tell him you think the relationship isn't going to make it.

c.   Tell him you are in for the duration, but these problems need to be fixed.

9. **When you feel he has done something really wrong to you, you**

   a. Yell or nastily tell him everything you think of him, without holding back.
   b. Yell or are nasty, but hold back the worst things you can think of.
   c. Tell him why you are angry, describe the problems of the specific act and ask him to go with you to counseling if you think it's beyond the two of you to find a solution.

10. **You think he has been unfaithful to you. You**

   a. Tell him you are leaving, pure and simple.
   b. Find out what happened and then decide if you're going to leave.
   c. Find out what happened and try to find out what went wrong—you will, if you can, hold your marriage together.

SCORING

Give yourself zero points for every *a* response, two points for every *b* response and three points for every *c* response.

0–7 POINTS

You definitely have not found a way, as a couple, to deal with stress constructively. You act first, angrily, impulsively—or you block out issues and let them smolder. If you don't learn more couple skills, one of these times of stress may undermine your relationship entirely. Perhaps it already has. If so, go see a counselor and find out what can be reconstructed with the help of a third party.

8–16 POINTS

You communicate reasonably well and you try not to be malicious. Still, the two of you don't seem to have enough skills to handle really rough stuff. Look at your *a* and/or *b* responses and see why you should handle these scenarios differently.

17–23 POINTS

You do well together: You talk and negotiate and pull together as a team under most crisis situations. But there are still a few exceptions that can hurt you. Look at those questions and think about what you can do differently. Even one area of panic or punishment under highly stressful conditions can be very hurtful to your relationship.

24–30 POINTS

You do as well as human beings ought to be expected to do! After all, we all lose it occasionally when we are scared or stressed. But the two of you have figured out how to help and comfort each other—and solve problems.

ANALYSIS

1.   There are always disappointments in a relationship. And the blow is all the more devastating when expectation and anticipation have been high. If you've worked hard to make something special and it falls through, it's easy to get hostile and strike out, but of course that only punishes you both more. Partners who have their act together accept disappointment and start over again.

2.   Some partners use sex to self-soothe; to make the world all right again. Other partners cannot even think of sex when things are going wrong. There is no right or wrong way to handle this kind of stress—except that no person's style should be treated with disrespect. If you know your partner would feel better making love, don't give him a look that makes him feel like a creep. If you prefer to cuddle, talk about it. Explore each other's feelings and discuss what would make lovemaking feel right—and what would not.

3.   Sometimes a partner is a bad actor. It's easy to get angry at moodiness. It's fair to be unhappy that his first moment home is a display of anger. But this is exactly where a calm and caring approach really can dissipate stress. If you can be nonreactive—understanding that it really doesn't have anything to do with you—then the subsequent conversation will not escalate into mutual anger. You will be able to make a storm into a minimal dark cloud and you will feel good about your self-control and the wisdom and perspective you can give him. Once he calms down, he's going to be very appreciative too.

4.   There are many times in a relationship when someone is not where they are supposed to be. Your relationship will be full of stress if you imagine the worst every time he isn't on schedule or in place. But even if you don't imagine the worst, you can create more, not less, stress if you immediately start trying to find out where he is and what he is doing. The best response is to give each other a little slack and a lot of trust. Give your partner the credit to have a good reason for his change of plans. Most of the time nothing is wrong. Save your emergency reactions for true emergencies.

5.   Money worries are hard on relationships. It's easy to get so scared that you start blaming each other or leap to extreme responses

like selling the house and moving to a small apartment in Tijuana. Better way: Remember that, no matter what, the two of you are in this together, and you are not the first people who ever spent more than they should have. Talk rationally about possible strategies, and resist pointing any fingers. Solve this as a couple, and your relationship will be the stronger for it.

6.   Supressing sadness inside is alienating. Plus, partners want to feel needed, so they need to know why their partners are unhappy. On the other hand, letting all your feelings suddenly explode can be overwhelming, and a partner may not know how to respond. Share stress from the beginning; let a partner know what is making you anxious or unhappy. Even better: Be specific about how to support you.

7.   Partners need permission to fail or do something wrong and know that their partner will understand and not punish them for screwing up. But you need to trust your partner enough to tell him bad news in order to find out if he can handle it! Furthermore, in a serious situation, hiding things from your partner is not only going to heighten your stress, it will probably lead to a worse outcome of the problem.

8.   The worst stressor is pulling the "I'm leaving you" card when a fight gets going. The next worse move is giving the impression that all is hopeless, even if leaving isn't imminent. A couple can reduce stress, even under a lot of pressure, by vowing that however bad the fight, the goal in mind is always to work things out rather than leave. You can handle the stress of even the nastiest exchange of feelings if at the outset you know that divorce or separation is not on the table.

9.   Really tough times in the relationship can pull you apart—or pull you closer—it all depends. If you unload and say anything you

feel, it's going to have a destructive effect (see Quiz Number 24, "Do You Fight Fair?"). On the other hand, if you hold back the information your partner needs to know about what is really making you mad, there is no way of solving things and becoming closer. That's why the only really good answer is *c*: Make it clear what the problem is and get professional help if you cannot manage honesty without nastiness. Then there is the possibility of change.

10.   Some people think that the biggest stressor a couple can experience is an extramarital affair. No one wants to think about it or believe it can happen. If it does, is there a way to handle it that would allow the relationship to survive? Obviously, if the only reaction that seems possible is immediately leaving (or making him leave) then there is no possibility for understanding and healing. Listening to the facts is a first step toward seeing if something is temporarily rather than terminally wrong in the relationship and if trust and love can be restored. Partners who can reconfigure their relationship after this kind of breach might live to be thankful that they gave the relationship another chance.

Does Your Relationship Pass the Honesty Test?

♥

We all revere honesty, but most of us pay lip service to the idea that truth is essential to a healthy relationship. But do we really want to know *everything* about a significant other—and share everything about ourselves as well? Are there times when modifying or even omitting a few facts is appropriate? Answer these questions to see where you draw the line.

1. **You just bought the coolest pair of knee-high boots ever created. Problem is, they cost practically a week's paycheck and you feel a bit sheepish about it. You**

    a. Fess up to your partner about the actual amount you shelled out, even though you expect a lecture.
    b. Proudly model your boots for your partner, but knock a few dollars off the price tag when he asks how much they cost.
    c. Put the box out with the recycling when your partner isn't

home, and tell him you found the amazing pair at the local thrift shop.

2. **Your partner is wearing a green-and-yellow checked shirt and you hate it with a passion. When he asks for your thumbs-up on his outfit, you**

    a. Tell him the shirt is beyond ugly. Why should you suppress your real feelings?

    b. Admit that you'd prefer he change into something slightly hipper, but only if he isn't attached to this particular shirt.

    c. Reassure him that he looks great—even if you don't think so. Why not make him feel good?

3. **When discussing your past lovers with your man, you**

    a. Tell him about the important relationships in some detail. He should know everything about you, right?

    b. Share quite a bit but downplay how important any past lovers were, compared to him.

    c. Omit—or modify—certain elements of your past. You don't want to upset him, make him jealous or have him think negatively of you.

4. **You've done something you're not particularly proud of, such as open a letter not addressed to you that you know you shouldn't touch. You**

    a. Tell your partner the whole story in the hope that he'll ease your guilt, help you out of the situation or tell you why you screwed up.

    b. Tell your mate a version of the truth that's not hugely unflattering to you. After all, you *do* want to get the guilt off your chest, but you don't want him to think horribly of you.

   c.   Decide to keep the whole thing under wraps.

5. **You're lounging in the park with your guy when you spy a very attractive dude playing with his puppy. You**

   a.   Share your attraction with your man, even though you worry it might peeve him.

   b.   Tell your guy to check out the hottie with the Scottie. You're pretty sure it won't bother him.

   c.   Keep your lip zipped (but if you must, sneak peeks when your partner is distracted by something else).

6. **Does your partner have any idea what you *really* talk about with your best girlfriends?**

   a.   Yes. You tell your man exactly what you and your friends talk about.

   b.   Sort of. You give your partner the cleaned-up version of what you and your friends spill.

   c.   No way! You never share privileged girl talk.

7. **Your partner wants you to accompany him to a bowl-a-thon with his officemates. You'd just as soon do the laundry. You**

   a.   Tell your partner you're really not into the "work-outing" thing, and would prefer to stay in.

   b.   Tell your guy that if it weren't for your other plans (a white lie) you'd go, even though you really don't like to bowl.

   c.   Tell him you love bowling (you hate it) but that you have big plans (you don't). In short, lie from start to finish.

8. **When your partner does something in bed that doesn't feel particularly good, you**

   a. Tell him he's not quite pressing your love button, then show him what *really* gets you hot and bothered.

   b. Whisper to him that he's the best, but subtly try to get him to do something else by guiding his hands and lips with yours.

   c. Moan, thrash, bite your lip: Do everything in your power to pump up his ego (and get the moment over with as quickly as possible).

9. One of your guy's best friends is a real jerk. You

   a. Tell your man exactly that—and explain why.

   b. Tell your partner that Joe Loser isn't your favorite friend, but don't reveal the depth of your dislike.

   c. Don't say a word. If your partner likes him, how bad could he be?

10. You've been unfaithful to your partner, or you've wanted to be. You

   a. Share all infidelities (of both body and mind) with your mate.

   b. Hide your dirty deeds but share your wandering thoughts freely.

   c. Conceal any thoughts that might suggest you have sexual desires elsewhere.

SCORING

MOSTLY A'S

Nothing but the Truth

While your honest ways may build trust and intimacy, you may sometimes cross the line into hurtful criticism. If you're always blunt with your honey—whether on the subject of his taste in clothes or his lovemaking skills—you'd better hope that he's a confident guy who loves you for your bold ways. Otherwise, he might go looking for a less-daunting match. Remember: It's not wrong or less loving to keep your thoughts to yourself once in a while.

MOSTLY B'S

Sometimes You're Honest; Sometimes You're Not

You have an innate sensitivity about when to be brutally honest and when to sugarcoat things. In general, you go for the truth (except when you think you'll hurt your partner's feelings or jeopardize the relationship). You use truth constructively, which is smart, since complete honesty is more than most egos—and relationships—can handle.

MOSTLY C'S

Liar, Liar!

You've got a lot going on that your partner doesn't know about. It's also likely that you feel kind of lonely with your guy, because you're keeping so much to yourself. It's okay to protect your partner from some information—a little privacy is not a bad thing; but if you're hiding all of your important issues, the two of you can't grow as a couple. And if you're trapped in a pattern of deceit, you might want to consider going for counseling to learn how to share, negotiate and trust.

ANALYSIS

1. The Spending Lie

Many women, especially those who aren't bringing home a salary, do a little creative repricing when it comes to discretionary purchases. It's not entirely honest, but it's not particularly destructive, either. Still, you might want to think about why you fudge the financial truth. Are you worried that your partner thinks you're flaky about money? Do you resent that you don't have more fiscal independence or privacy? These may be issues you need to address in order to solidify your relationship.

2. The Fashion Fib

On the one hand, your partner wants and needs an honest evaluation of his ensemble so that he can look his best. On the other, harsh criticism can hurt, making your partner feel self-conscious and less than attractive. A better option than absolute honesty: Tell him your true feelings about what he's wearing only when he's dressing for an important event or if he's clearly ambivalent about the outfit.

3. The Life-Before-Him Lie

Sure, talking about former loves can help your current main squeeze understand who you are and what shaped you. However, your love tales could sound like bragging and stir up jealousies and fears that may ultimately undermine a healthy relationship. Of course, some men are truly interested in a rundown of your history for the best reason—they want to know you. If that's the case, be honest. But if you suspect that your mate is a jealous or insecure type who will obsess about measuring up and be suspicious every time you talk to another guy, telling the truth will only bring you misery. The best bet in that instance: Underplay everything—or say nothing at all.

4. Daring to Bare Your Insecurities

Being honest is hard when you're in the wrong, but it's essential to a close relationship. Ideally, your partner should be the one person you can run to when you've screwed up, so that you can get support and insight about how to do better next time around. If you opt out of sharing, you may be feeling insecure about being truly loved and lovable (which is something to pay attention to). Another possibility: You suspect that your partner is incapable of giving you the emotional support you need.

5.   The Secrets of Attraction

Keep your wandering eye to yourself, unless ogling cuties together is something that turns you both on. For most people, showing interest in someone else is a surefire way to stir up a partner's jealousy. If that's the case, don't disclose. If you must make your feelings known, keep the comments short and sweet. Your partner doesn't need to hear you going on and on about your attraction.

6.   The Truth About Girl Gossip

Most men would be shocked to learn how much their partners' friends know about them—everything from how they behave during an argument to how they perform in the sack. That said, it's probably best not to reveal exactly how much you dish to your pals, unless you're willing to risk your mate's feeling exposed or betrayed. Either play down the extent of the talk or be quietly mysterious about it.

7.   The What-You-Like Lie

It's generally best to be honest about what you do and don't enjoy. (If you lie about your preferences, you may wind up bowling a lot!) Besides, constant excuses breed suspicion. Better to come clean and go your separate ways for the evening.

8.   To Fake or Not to Fake

Too many men never get adequate feedback from their lovers. The end result? Lots of unnecessary dissatisfaction between the sheets. If you're worried about hurting his feelings, remember that honesty tempered with kindness and some subtle direction is essential to the long-term quality of your sex life.

9. Fair-weather Friends

No, you shouldn't have to hang out with someone you really dislike. But since friends are often seen as an extension of one's own identity, if you attack a mate's buddy, you're pretty much attacking your mate. The bottom line: Don't expound on the full extent of your distaste. Instead, say just enough so that you'll have to spend only a moderate amount of time with that particular friend of his.

10. The Fidelity Fib

If you've been unfaithful (or truly crave someone else), admitting it can be deadly to your relationship. While relationships *can* survive an affair, it takes a very strong couple to bounce back from that kind of betrayal, and the paranoia and pain can take years to abate. Remember, though, there's a difference between being slightly drawn to your next-door neighbor and thinking constantly about having an affair—or actually going ahead and doing the deed. If the latter is happening and you think you want out of your relationship, it could be time for the truth. The shock might make you two reevaluate things and motivate you to rebuild your intimacy.

Do You Want to Find a Sugar Daddy or Be a Trophy Wife?

♥

Ah, be careful what you wish for . . . you might get it. On the other hand, maybe this bargain is for you.

Respond TRUE or FALSE.

1. I wouldn't mind putting in two to four hours a day on body maintenance.

2. One of the saddest things in the world is a broken nail.

3. I love the idea that my man's main obsession with me is my looks.

4. I don't mind having to travel with my husband at a moment's notice.

5. I love getting expensive presents, even if my husband expects excessive compliments and sex on demand in return.

6. I am not at all insecure. So what if he is looking at a woman who is prettier than I am?

7. I don't mind not making my own money. I am not nervous about being totally dependent on the money my husband gives me.

8. I love men with king-size egos.

9. I would get breast augmentation and other plastic surgeries if my man wanted me to.

10. To be honest, there is nothing more important to me in marriage than being truly rich.

SCORING

Give yourself one point for each TRUE response.

0–3 POINTS

You are *not* a trophy wife! Try it, and I see a divorce around the corner. You might like a few of the perks or be flexible on one or two items, but basically you are going to think this guy is a jerk, and you will be unable to meet his demands. Pay your own way, keep your freedom and leave your breasts the way they are.

4–7 POINTS

You are thinking about it. You are a material girl and you'd make a few sacrifices for being taken care of. Still, you have your limits—and sugar daddies don't really like limits very much. As a trophy wife you'd have a little more clout (you'd be *so* expensive to divorce) but remember, he has the money to hire *very* nasty lawyers. . . .

8–10 POINTS

Go for it! You were made for this job. A lot of women might get upset and think he was too piggy to live with—but you just consider it a fair cost of doing business. You might prefer being in love—and be lucky enough to find someone whom you *do* love who is *also* capable of being a sugar daddy or trophy-wife seeker—but love is secondary here. Key words are *luxury*, *money*, maybe *power* and *fame*. Don't forget those endless spa and upkeep appointments—not paid for by you. You know what you want—can't say that for everyone!

Do You Fight Fair?

♥ ────

Sure, you fight—about money, sex, his dirty socks on the floor or your damp stockings hanging in the bathtub. Fighting is perfectly normal, and it doesn't mean your relationship is doomed. It's how you *handle* these fights that predicts whether you'll be together for the long haul. Take this quiz to see if you're a prizefighter or a playground bully.

Respond TRUE or FALSE.

1. Arguing stresses me out, so when we fight, I usually withdraw and hide my real feelings.

2. I think expressing negativity just makes things worse.

3. I have trouble sticking to the issue at hand and often bring up things from the past that have annoyed me. After all, we're fighting!

4. I'm always analyzing my guy's personality and pointing out things that upset me. For example, I say things such as, "If you weren't so stubborn, this never would have happened!"

5. When we argue, I often feel about one millisecond away from exploding.

6. I wait until I'm 100 percent certain that I am right about an issue before bringing it up.

7. When I get *really* mad, the insults fly.

8. When we argue, I often feel disgusted with my partner—and I let him know it.

9. If my partner criticizes me for something, I reciprocate by telling him how *he* falls short.

10. When my partner doesn't seem to get what I'm saying during an argument, I'll repeat my point several times.

11. I admit it: Sometimes during an argument I'm barely listening to my partner, because I'm too busy thinking about my next retort.

12. I feel as if we have the same fight over and over.

SCORING

Give yourself one point for each TRUE response.

0–4 POINTS

You're a lover, not a fighter. Sure, you fight—but you do it right. Chances are that your relationship is going along swimmingly, and when you hit a bump, you have the tools to smooth things over.

Judging by your quiz results, you and your mate are stellar fighters.

5–8 POINTS

You fight right—sometimes. You've developed some strong fighting skills, but unfortunately, you lose sight of these (and your temper) in the heat of the moment—and that can overshadow the good stuff.

9–12 POINTS

You're a lean, mean, fighting machine. Let's just say that fighting isn't your strong point. You and your partner could probably benefit from seeing a therapist to help you sort out your quarreling quandaries. Chances are, you'll be amazed—and comforted—by how much both of you could gain from some fair-fighting tips.

ANALYSIS

1. A FALSE response indicates that you fight fair. Refusing to show your emotions can be as hurtful to a relationship as constant bickering. While it may seem impressive to say, "We never fight," being in a don't-ask, don't-tell relationship causes negative feelings to fester.

2. The reasoning that negativity will only hurt a relationship seems perfectly logical, except that if your partner doesn't know what's in your head and heart, there won't be an opportunity to make things better. So bring up the tough stuff. The short-term pain is worth the longer-term gain.

3.   As soon as you utter the words, "You always do this," or, "You never do that," you're setting yourself up for an even bigger argument, peppered with accusatory statements such as, "Oh yeah? What about that time ten years ago when . . ." and, "If that's the way you see me, why should we bother with this relationship?" Sweeping condemnations and grudge-holding will get you nowhere. A better idea: Stick to whatever it is you're fighting about at the moment, and focus on each other's actions.

4.   It's tempting, though unproductive, to resort to faultfinding. But while it's fine—and even necessary—to complain about something your partner does (or doesn't do), when you go after *who he is*, you're inviting an angry, defensive response. Save the heart-to-heart about each other's personality flaws for a time when you're both in a supportive frame of mind.

5.   If you're really going to blow your top, one of two things is happening: (a) You've waited too long to deal with your anger; or (b) You've got anger-management issues. If it's the former, by the time you 'fess up to your real feelings, you're too upset to be rational. If you typically have a hard time dealing with anger (you lose your temper instantaneously, shout, hit or leave—none of which is fair and one of which is illegal), your chances of solving your problems plummet. Learn how to recognize when you are about to lose it (your pulse quickens, your heart pounds, you get red in the face) and excuse yourself until you can approach the issue like the mature, reasonable person you want to be.

6.   To get to the bottom of any disagreement, you have to be willing to figure out your role in causing the problem. If you assume you're always right, you'll have trouble hearing your mate's point of view. In a truly fair fight, each person has a chance to win (or at least to make a few points).

7.   If you call your partner names, something is wrong between you that may eventually unravel your relationship. You need to learn how to disagree without being hurtful. (Hint: Couples therapy can help.)

8.   Does rolling your eyes, smirking at his remarks or laughing derisively at his points sound familiar? If it does, it has to stop. Mutual respect has to be demonstrated or nothing constructive can take place. Contempt can be lethal to a relationship.

9.   Counterattacks don't resolve anything, even if your come-back is technically accurate. The next time you find yourself putting your partner down, try taking a deep breath, and then consider the complaint and address it.

10.   You may think that you're just trying to explain yourself, but face it: Your guy isn't likely to find your argument any more compelling the fifth time.

11.   If you pretend to be listening, and your partner can tell that you're not, that will just stoke his resentment. A better way to fight: Listen first, then share your feelings and try to respond to what your mate said. Otherwise, he may stop taking part in discussions altogether.

12.   If you responded TRUE, the two of you really haven't found an effective way to resolve your differences. If you never make progress on important issues, your relationship is in danger. It's important for a couple to feel that they understand each other and can work out their problems.

Are You Cheating
(and Don't Know It)?

♥

You're firmly committed to your significant other. You'd never kiss another guy, much less do the nasty. Even so, betraying the person you love doesn't always require crossing a physical boundary. Answer the following questions to see if your heart is *really* true.

Respond TRUE or FALSE.

While in a committed relationship with a romantic partner, you have

1. Made a beeline for the most attractive guest at a cocktail party and proceeded to turn on the charm.

2. Chatted with someone who was very much your type and then daydreamed about what it would be like to make love with him.

3. Fantasized about a mysterious stranger while having sex with your partner.

4. Fantasized during lovemaking about your officemate, your next-door neighbor or someone else.

5. Told someone you had a sexual fantasy about them.

6. Regularly turned to an attractive male friend to confide your deepest wishes and problems.

7. Exchanged slightly flirtatious e-mails with a cyber someone you've never met in person.

8. Exchanged daily or weekly romantic e-mails with a certain cyber friend you've never met in person.

9. Had phone (or cyber) sex with someone you've never met.

10. Kissed someone other than your partner (and we don't mean on the cheek!).

11. Let someone besides your partner touch your breasts.

12. Come dangerously close to making love with someone other than your mate.

SCORING

1. TRUE = 1 point   FALSE = 0 points
2. TRUE = 1 point   FALSE = 0 points
3. TRUE = 1 point   FALSE = 0 points

4.	TRUE = 2 points	FALSE = 0 points
5.	TRUE = 2 points	FALSE = 0 points
6.	TRUE = 2 points	FALSE = 0 points
7.	TRUE = 2 points	FALSE = 0 points
8.	TRUE = 7 points	FALSE = 0 points
9.	TRUE = 7 points	FALSE = 0 points
10.	TRUE = 7 points	FALSE = 0 points
11.	TRUE = 10 points	FALSE = 0 points
12.	TRUE = 10 points	FALSE = 0 points

0–3 POINTS

Your heart is true. You've been known to engage in your share of flirtatious banter with handsome strangers or to occasionally dream of a romantic romp with the postman. So what? A little erotic imagination isn't disloyal, and you may even be able to channel that sexual energy right back into your committed relationship.

4–7 POINTS

You're restless at heart. By letting someone other than your beau know that he stirs your blood (or by reserving one person as your go-to fantasy guy), you've opened the door to emotional disloyalty, even if you never intend to act on your fantasies. Truth is, you have a wayward heart, and if you care about your current relationship, it makes sense to think about the factors that are causing you to turn away from the one you love.

8–11 POINTS

Your heart beats for others. No, you haven't been physically intimate with anyone but your mate, but you have certainly crossed a line, intimacy-wise. Your partner would surely be hurt were he to learn about your wanderings. If you're concerned about truly being faithful, you need to establish stricter boundaries with the other men in your life.

12–20 POINTS

Your heart is on the run. Whether over the Internet or in your hotel room on a business trip, you've been romantically and sexually linked to someone other than your partner. If your partner did this to you, what would you call it?

21 OR MORE POINTS

You have a cheating heart. If you've had any sexual contact with someone other than your partner, you're in cheating territory. Period. (Ditto if you're involved in an ongoing virtual romance.)

Should You Stay or Should You Go?

♥

Every relationship has its ups and downs, but how long does it have to be down before it's time to give the whole thing up? People torture themselves with this decision. "Should I try harder?" "Is this a losing proposition?" It's not always clear. Answer these 15 questions to help you decide if it's *really* over.

Respond TRUE or FALSE.

1. The way he slurps his pasta, the way he takes snore-heavy catnaps, the rumpled flannel shirt he wears every Saturday—they used to be endearing; now they're annoying.

2. When an important thing happens—friend turmoil, a career change, a medical scare—you find yourself preferring to talk about it with almost anyone *but* your partner.

3. You can't quite say "I love you" anymore.

4. Romantic, loving sex is a distant memory. These days, sex is either rare or feels more like an obligation than a pleasure.

5. You still try to create intimate moments—whether it's dinner for two or flipping off the TV and chatting about each other's day.

6. You and your beau may be having problems, but you still feel respected.

7. If your partner isn't grabbing drinks with buddies after work, you're staying late at the office or sneaking in a bite with some friends before heading home.

8. When you and your partner go out, you no longer have that look-who's-with-me sense of pride.

9. Your glacial silences and snide comments to each other have escalated. Sometimes you even say nasty things about each other in front of your kids, family or friends.

10. You've fantasized about leaving (and have even gone so far as to figure out ways to afford it, or to consider what it *really* would be like to live alone).

11. If you were officially single and picking a partner today, you wouldn't choose the person you're with now.

12. If you share a home with your partner, the atmosphere is generally cold, angry or conflicted.

13. You're depressed and feel unloved, unloving or both.

14. The financial costs of leaving your partner—which in the past have made you hesitate to go—seem less daunting now.

15. You're actively in a relationship on the side—sexual or not—that's more satisfying than your present partner.

SCORING

Give yourself one point for each of these responses.

1. TRUE
2. TRUE
3. TRUE
4. TRUE
5. FALSE
6. FALSE
7. TRUE
8. FALSE
9. TRUE
10. TRUE
11. TRUE
12. TRUE
13. TRUE
14. TRUE
15. TRUE

0–2 POINTS

You're still on solid ground. You aren't going anywhere just yet. You may have a few issues, but it doesn't sound as though they amount to anything that a little attention and recommitment couldn't cure.

3–8 POINTS

You've got some pretty heavy-duty problems, but also some impressive strengths. There's hope for your partnership. Look at each issue seriously and start taking steps to correct the things that are undermining your relationship.

9–12 POINTS

There aren't many positive feelings left in your relationship. If you think about the cost-to-benefit ratio and there is still somewhat of a bright side, then you and your partner should invest in some therapy (or a new therapist).

13–15 POINTS

If your bags aren't already packed, they probably should be. It doesn't sound as though there's much left in your relationship. Maybe one last-ditch effort at counseling would help.

Are You Ready to Have a Baby?

♥

Lately, thoughts of tiny fingers and toes, bottles and bassinets have been dancing in your head. Does this mean you're ready to leave your freewheeling, always-ready-for-a-party lifestyle to become a parent? Or have you just attended one too many baby showers? Answer these 12 questions to see if you're truly ready to reproduce.

1. **Once your theoretical bundle of joy arrives, how will you and your partner divvy up the parenting?**

   a. From nursing to nursery rhymes, it'll be me all the way.
   b. My partner will pitch in whenever possible, but I expect to shoulder the bulk of the baby duties.
   c. I'm shooting to share parenting as much as possible.
   d. I haven't quite found a father-to-be yet.

2. **You've settled in for a long, transatlantic flight home, when a mom and crying baby slip into the seat next to you. What's your reaction?**

   a. I offer to help the clearly worn-out mom.
   b. I desperately ring for the flight attendant to see if I can make a last-minute seat change.
   c. I stay put, but fume silently. Constant crying drives me up the wall.
   d. Cluck sympathetically, then don my earphones and bury my nose in a big book.

3. **How long have you been with your co-parent-to-be?**

   a. Less than a year.
   b. Two years.
   c. Three years or more.
   d. I'm not currently in a serious relationship.

4. **How will a baby change your relationship?**

   a. The new addition will create more intimacy in our marriage.
   b. Sharing a child will make our sexual connection more intense.
   c. Having a baby will finally seal our commitment.
   d. A new baby will present some relationship hurdles but will ultimately bring us closer.

5. **Pretend you're seven months pregnant—complete with swollen belly, wild mood swings and salt cravings. What would you do if the opportunity to take a free (and fabulous) foreign excursion came up?**

a.   I would go—a European jaunt would be just what I would need.

b.   I would pass, regretfully. I wouldn't want anything, like a potentially germ-filled ventilation system, to get in the way of a healthy delivery.

c.   I would nix the offer without a second thought.

6.   The idea of a stinky diaper

a.   Makes me want to hand the little darling straight to someone else.

b.   Makes me queasy.

c.   Makes me realize that I, too, will find myself having discussions about poop.

d.   Has never once crossed my mind.

7.   Have you and your partner talked about what you would do if your child is born with serious mental or physical challenges?

a.   Yes. We've discussed it and have come to a mutual agreement about how we would deal with it.

b.   No, but I assume we would keep the baby at home no matter what.

c.   No, but I assume we would put the child in an appropriate facility outside the home.

8.   How's your financial health?

a.   Poor. I'm pretty much living paycheck to paycheck.

b.   Pretty good. I've banked just enough to pay bills, with some left over for fun.

c.   Excellent. I've got plenty of cash for the fun stuff, though I haven't gotten around to saving much yet.

d. Excellent. Cash flow is not a concern, and I've put away a tidy sum in savings and investments.

9. How would you rate your sex life?

a. Not particularly steamy.
b. Satisfying for both of us.
c. Excellent, but more important to my husband than to me.
d. Not great. One (or both) of us is dissatisfied.

10. When discussing the future, what have you and your partner touched on?

a. Saving for our kids' education.
b. The role religion will play in our family.
c. How we would discipline our little ones.
d. All of the above.

11. How do you envision your parenting style?

a. My partner and I would both be pretty liberal (or both pretty strict).
b. One of us would be permissive and the other would be strict.
c. I have no idea.

12. How does the idea of being pregnant make you feel?

a. I cringe. I'm not at all looking forward to the weight gain, the mood swings or the unfashionable maternity wear.
b. Excited—though I'm a tad nervous that I won't be able to get my pre-baby body back.
c. Excited—I can't wait to see what this phase of life feels like.

SCORING

Give yourself one point for each of these responses.

1. c
2. a
3. c
4. d
5. c
6. c
7. a
8. d
9. b
10. d
11. a
12. c

0–4 POINTS

Put on the baby brakes! You may *think* you want a bundle to coo at and cuddle with, but your score says you haven't really thought this through. Kids inevitably require major changes, compromises and sacrifices (physical, emotional and financial), and you have to be ready. Otherwise, you may end up with a little bundle—of regrets!

5–8 POINTS

You're nearly baby-ready. You're itching to multiply, but there are a few details that still need to be ironed out before you aim to conceive. Life post-baby (as wonderful as it is) is stressful—and your relationship and sexual habits definitely won't feel the same for a while. Planning can help get you and your mate through those potentially bumpy few months more easily, as can having realistic expectations about what a baby can do for you—and your relationship.

9–12 POINTS

Oh, baby! You're ready to go. You and your partner have given having children some serious thought and you're both on the same page. Good for you. Now all you need to do is get down to the baby-making.

Do You Have Any of the Twelve Worst Problems of Marriage?

♥

All marriages have problems. But there are twelve pitfalls that are particularly common and destructive. This quiz will help you identify whether or not your relationship suffers from any or many of these vulnerabilities. If you find out any bad news, the good news is now that you recognize what is going on, you can do something about it!

Respond TRUE or FALSE.

1. We don't talk about our deepest hopes, fears, goals and feelings.

2. Each of us is so busy and we have so little time together that I often feel we are not in the same life together.

3. My partner sometimes rolls his eyes when I speak, or ridicules what I do. Or I do that to him.

4. I don't think we have done anything new and interesting together in a long time.

5. I feel taken for granted.

6. My partner doesn't go out of his way to do me favors or buy me gifts.

7. I do most of the housework and/or child care, and I feel this is unfair.

8. I feel like I am under my partner's thumb. Or I feel physically and/or emotionally abused.

9. We don't show each other much affection, sexual or otherwise, anymore.

10. We have problems that never get solved.

11. We strongly disagree about having children. Or we disagree about how to discipline the children.

12. We argue about money a lot.

SCORING

Give yourself one point for each TRUE response.

0 POINTS

What? You think no one can get a zero on this test? You are absolutely wrong. Great relationships have *none* of these problems. If you scored a zero, congratulations. Yours is a model of what marriage can be if you are fair and loving, and if you work at it. I want to put you on television or send you around the country talking about how you do it. Everyone needs to know that long-term relationships *can* remain intimate, equitable, respectful and loving.

1–3 POINTS

You're in a thriving relationship. But even a couple of points on this quiz points out weaknesses. It would be worth your while to read about the items you marked TRUE. See what you can do about them, so your relationship remains rewarding and secure.

4–7 POINTS

You've got more problems than are safe for a long-term relationship. You may be intact as a couple, but you're not very happy. These problems may be more than you can handle—you definitely may benefit from seeing a counselor.

8–12 POINTS

Your relationship is in big trouble and you must be very unhappy about it. There are too many important issues for you to handle by yourself. If you aren't already seeing a therapist, you should be. It looks like respect and connection has eroded and the two of you are building separate lives. All is not necessarily lost if you take your situation seriously and decide to do something about it. Read further: Hopefully the following analysis will help convince you that things should be fixed—and also, that it is worth it to try!

ANALYSIS

1.   Failing to Maintain Communication

Falling in love is all about communication. *Maintaining* love absolutely needs communication. Sometimes couples make the unfortunate mistake of handling daily tasks as if they fulfill the communication requirement; sooner or later this feels really empty. Intimacy is built not just by organizing the car pool or a dinner party together, but by having moments alone with each other to thoughtfully consider life and its meaning. Teamwork is built by rethinking or reaffirming goals, and by feeling the better for having had this experience. If conversation seems never more than utilitarian, one (or both) of you feels lonely. Get connected before hurt and resentful feelings cause a break, an affair or depression.

2.   Living Parallel Lives

There is nothing really wrong with the relationship—except that it isn't much of a relationship. Partner A is busy taking the kids to school, helping the kids with their homework, organizing church efforts for the homeless and taking care of invalid grandparents. Partner B is trying to build a small business, traveling a lot or staying late at the office and takes Saturdays to finally have a day on the golf course or play with the kids. Partner A catches up on errands on Saturdays. Only Sunday is left as a family day, but somehow that too gets eaten up by social obligations and family chores. No one is yelling at anyone else, but sometimes couples like this can't quite remember why they are married to each other. Of course, all relationships have periods like this, but if it goes on for years, watch out!

3.   The Low Blow of Contempt

Contempt is the most dangerous thing that can happen in a relationship. One partner no longer respects the other and, in small or large ways, they show it. There are snide remarks, cutting condemnations or condescending looks. Contempt is so destructive that psychologist John Gottman, a well-respected researcher on marriage, says that it is one of the most important signs that a marriage is going to end. If a marriage has come to this much loss of respect it is in trouble and needs help.

4. Falling Into Boredom
Spouses can bore each other into oblivion. Marriages have to be about fun and personal growth as much as they are about caring for children, earning a living or achieving security. If life feels humdrum, partners start feeling they are missing all the good stuff. Women miss romance, men miss passion and both men and women can long for travel, adventure and something new. It is really common for couples to fall into a rut—but it's not inevitable and it's not good for a marriage.

5. Taking Your Partner for Granted
Everybody needs appreciation. A good cook needs to hear how much those meals mean to everyone. When partners look especially good, they want to be noticed; even everyday personality characteristics, like a good sense of humor or organizational skills, require appreciation. Otherwise, partners get resentful and sad—and if a third party enters the picture and notices all those forgotten qualities, it is a head turner. No one should feel that his or her wonderful qualities are no longer noticed or given credit.

6. The Loss of Generosity and Thoughtfulness
Gifts touch the heart. When people first court, there are all sorts of sweet things exchanged, just because couples who are in love enjoy pleasing each other. The cost of a gift is unimportant: What matters is showing someone that he is on your mind and you want to do something nice for him. If this has stopped, it means that courtship has

stopped—but you should never stop trying to win your partner's heart. A marriage that has stopped saying "I love you," in various ways, is fragile.

7. The Loss of Fairness

Housework is one of the most common battlefields of the American marriage. The fight is not just about who does the dishes—that's just the subject, not the real issue. The real issues are equity, fairness, respect and helpfulness. Most men do not do their fair share of housework; just about every study ever done shows that. The issues are more about what they contribute, how much they do pitch in, and if it seems equitable and caring to the other partner. Women, in particular, want to feel like a team member, not a servant.

8. Being Over-controlled or Emotionally or Physically Abused

If a partner feels dominated or, even worse, if there is physical or mental abuse, the marriage is in a shambles. Even if the marriage looks good from the outside, fear and resentment are the backstage themes. It would be great if this weren't in the top twelve things that can go wrong in a marriage, but sadly, abuse is very common. It can range from isolating a woman from her friends, making her feel that she is worthless and untrustworthy, to getting beaten up. Subtler forms of intimidation and domination are also destructive to love and happiness, such as not being allowed any independence, being criticized all the time, or not having access to money.

9. The Loss of Romance and Sexuality

If the two of you feel more like roommates and less like lovers, you have a common but still dangerous pattern in your relationship. Holding hands and other small endearments keep romance alive and are necessary for couples to feel physically bonded. But if that's *all* you do, it won't be enough for a lot of marriages. A sluggish sex life may be tolerable, but an absent one usually has at least one partner feeling deprived, disappointed and angry. It is easy to become less physical over time and it may be hard to reinstitute without some counseling. Still, renewing that spark is not impossible, and there is no doubt that its presence makes a marriage stronger.

10.   The Problem of Continuous or Unresolved Anger
Marital therapists have found that a common central characteristic of unhappy or unstable marriages is that disagreements may get put away but never solved. The couple does not feel the marriage is vital or viable because arguments never change anything. If you have not resolved most of your big issues (and many small ones), there is likely to be a feeling of being unsuited for each other. Problems and conflict do not undermine a relationship as much as people think they do. Never facing them squarely or dealing with them is the issue.

11.   Conflicts Over the Kids
The desire to have children is a passionate one. If someone who really wants children agrees not to have them, that decision may come back to haunt the relationship. More commonly, the big battles are about whether and how to discipline kids when they have misbe-haved. Permissive individuals coupled with strict partners can get into intense arguments unless they find a system of negotiation and compromise. When people fight about what is good for their children, they tend not to back down. Couples need a common value system, or it can be toxic for the whole family.

12.   Money Matters
If a partner's economic expectations and hopes have been dashed, there is the possibility of blame-placing and bitterness. Even if there is enough money most of the time, partners who are in a boom-and-bust cycle have to have nerves of steel not to get upset with each other. Insecurity usually brings out the worst in people, and eco-nomic insecurity is no different. Money is often a control issue, and if

the partner who earns less is dictated to by the person who earns more, a struggle for equality can take place. Then there are all those other chances for disagreement—how much to spend on who or what, how much to save or how much to donate to charity. Different goals and money styles can drive a deep wedge between partners.

What you need to

know about building

a great sex life

♥

Rate Your Sex I.Q.

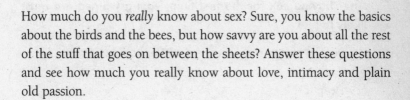

How much do you *really* know about sex? Sure, you know the basics about the birds and the bees, but how savvy are you about all the rest of the stuff that goes on between the sheets? Answer these questions and see how much you really know about love, intimacy and plain old passion.

1. The corona is

    a. The most sexually sensitive part of a man's body.
    b. The area between the scrotum and the anus.
    c. The area around a man's nipple.

2. Who's having the most sex?

    a. Divorced men.
    b. Single men or women under the age of 30.
    c. Married couples.

3. What percentage of heterosexuals lose their virginity by age 19?

    a.   33 percent.

    b.   50 percent.

    c.   75–80 percent.

4. After having sex for the first time, young men are most likely to feel

    a.   Afraid that their partner will get pregnant and/or contract an STD.

    b.   Anxiety about performance.

    c.   Elation—they finally did it!

5. After having sex for the first time, young women are most likely to feel

    a.   Fearful of becoming pregnant and/or contracting an STD.

    b.   Guilt or regret.

    c.   Deep love.

6. What is the number-one reason young women have sex for the first time?

    a.   Curiosity.

    b.   Love or wanting to be loved.

    c.   Pressure or force from their boyfriends.

7. What is the number-one reason young men have sex for the first time?

    a.   Curiosity.

    b.   Love, or wanting to be loved.

    c.   Peer pressure.

8. What are the Lingam and Yoni?

    a. Sex toys.

    b. Terms used in Tantric sex.

    c. Sexual positions used in yoga.

9. Where is the "G spot"?

    a. In the lower wall of the vagina, about two inches in.

    b. In the upper wall of the vagina, about two inches in.

    c. Maybe nowhere—many experts don't think it exists.

10. What contraceptive is least likely to fail during a real-life sexual encounter (as opposed to a laboratory test of the contraceptive's effectiveness)?

    a. Cervical cap.

    b. The pill.

    c. Levonorgestrel implant (Norplant).

11. What is the average time a couple spends making love, from shedding their clothes to the post-coital cuddle?

    a. 15 minutes.

    b. A half hour.

    c. An hour.

12. The clitoris has

    a. Twice as many nerve endings as the penis.

    b. About half as many nerve endings as the penis.

    c. 100 times the nerve endings of the penis.

13. Which of these statements is true?

a. A woman can get pregnant during unprotected intercourse even if her male partner doesn't ejaculate.

b. A person can become infected with genital herpes by receiving oral sex from a partner who has herpes on his or her mouth.

c. More than 40 million sexually active adults have had human papilloma virus.

d. All of the above.

14. Ask a heterosexual man the number-one thing he would change about his partner and he is most likely to wish that she would

a. Be more adventurous in bed.

b. Initiate sex more often.

c. Achieve orgasms more easily.

15. Which sexual position provides the most clitoral stimulation?

a. Woman on knees, man behind.

b. Missionary Position #1: Male on top, on his knees; female on her back, with her legs open.

c. Missionary Position #2: Male on top with his legs fully extended; female on her back with her legs closed and extended straight out.

16. Of couples who have been together more than five years, who has the most sex?

a. Married couples.

b. Cohabiting couples.

c. Gay or lesbian couples.

17. **What percentage of people in the United States admit to having cheated on a partner?**

    a.   Between 10 and 20 percent.

    b.   About 33 percent.

    c.   About 54 percent.

SCORING

Give yourself one point for each of these responses.

  1. a

  2. c

  3. c

  4. b

  5. b

  6. b

  7. a

  8. b

  9. b or c

10. c

11. b

12. a

13. d

14. b

15. c

16. b

17. a

0–4 POINTS

You're a Sex Ed dropout! You need to brush up on the wheres and whys of the birds and the bees, not only for your own personal pleasure (and your partner's) but for your sexual health. Some good references: *All About Sex*, Three Rivers Press (Planned Parenthood's very good overview of sexually transmitted diseases, body processes and contraception) and *The Hormone Book* by Susan Love (a very frank and useful look into how hormones—or the lack of them—really affect women's bodies). I could go on—but these two books alone will triple your knowledge base.

5–11 POINTS

You're not as savvy as you think you are! No problem: a good reference book, like *Our Sexuality* or *Understanding Human Sexuality*, can bring you up to speed. Text authors I admire: Crooks and Baur, Debra Haffner, Hyde and Delamater, Sue Sprecher, Bob Kolodny, Ray Rosen and Sandra Leiblum. Any one of them will give you enough knowledge to authoritatively entertain at cocktail parties!

12–16 POINTS

You're a sexual smarty pants! You are a sex expert in disguise, especially when it comes to gauging male and female behavior. You also have a clear idea of how the human body works, and what men and women actually do with those bodies.

17 POINTS

You're a sexual genius! You *are* a sex researcher, aren't you? No one else would know this much. Whatever it is, you know how bodies work and what men and women actually do. I'm impressed. Congrats!

ANALYSIS

1. The corona—the ridge that completes the head of the penis—
is considered the most sexually sensitive part of the male body. Men
find oral or manual stimulation of this area particularly pleasurable.
But be careful: Just like the clitoris, if the corona is handled too
roughly over an extended period of time, it can become oversensitive
and prone to pain.

2. In general, married couples have the most sex (but see the
discussion and analysis of question 16). It's all logic: According to
The Social Organization of Sexuality, married couples have the most
continual access to each other, so they log more sack time. Ironically,
while being single may sound sexier, it usually isn't.

3. While the exact percentage sometimes varies from study to
study, most studies suggest that 75–80 percent of young men and
women have intercourse for the first time between the ages of 17 and
19. The mean age of first intercourse is about 16 for girls, 15 for
boys. The percentage of first-timers takes a leap during the junior
and senior years of high school and the first year of college or work.
Less than 20 percent of newlyweds in the United States are virgins on
their wedding night.

4. After having sex for the first time, young men are most
likely to feel anxiety about their performance. Sad to say, a guy's
first time is generally not joyful. The main first-time memory for
males is fear of failing to get an erection, losing an erection or inadequacy as a lover. Men report feeling relieved rather than thrilled.
The good news: Most do use contraception for the first time (about
60 percent), though men tend to fall off in contraceptive use there-
after.

5.   After having sex for the first time, young women are most likely to feel guilt or regret. Most young women, even when 100 percent willing, are still not emotionally ready for the experience of first-time sex. The majority report that they ended up having second thoughts, and most don't feel at ease with their choice. A sizable minority do feel positive about their decision to have sex, but in both groups, there is a great deal of ambivalence about whether they actually had an orgasm.

6.   The number-one reason young women decide to have sex for the first time is love or a desire to be loved. Most women are not coerced into their first sexual experience, nor do they lose their virginity while intoxicated. That's the good news. The bad news: Many young women say they had sex because they wanted to please their partner, not because they personally wanted to have intercourse. A sizable minority report having sex out of curiosity or lust.

7.   Curiosity is the number-one reason young men have sex for the first time. Guys have their first experience with sexual intercourse, more or less, simply to find out what the fuss is all about. And while this is not a particularly malicious motive, it sure is different from women, many of whom consider first-time sex a grand act of love. A sizable minority of young men, however, say that they had sex because they cared for their girlfriend.

8.   The Lingam and Yoni are the terms for the penis and vagina in Sanskrit Tantric texts. Tantric teachings enhance sexual pleasure by introducing rituals that intertwine spirituality and communication with sensuality. According to Tantra, the sexual act, if done right, can put you into a harmonious state with the universe. A nice introductory book (with great pictures!) is *The Art of Tantric Sex* by Nitya Lacroix.

9.   Many G spot believers subscribe to the theory that there is a *second* love button on a woman's body. It is located in the anterior

wall of the vagina and is actually a different sort of tissue than the rest of the vagina. Stimulating this spot results in extreme pleasure and, perhaps, female ejaculation. Penises, however, do not automatically reach this special spot. To get to it, a partner must either use fingers or a G spot stimulator. Many sex researchers, however, question the existence of the G spot altogether, contending that research has never confirmed that either the area or female ejaculation exists.

10.   Norplant, a device inserted into the upper arm by a health care professional, has the lowest real-life failure rate. According to research by Planned Parenthood, hormone-based contraceptive methods that don't require the sexually active person to remember to do something every day (e.g., take a pill) work the best. Norplant's active ingredient, progestin (a synthetic hormone similar to progesterone), prevents ovaries from releasing eggs. Though there have been problems with inserting and removing the device, when it comes to effectiveness, it's the hands-down winner, followed closely by Depo-Provera (and probably by other new hormonal methods now being introduced). Norplant can remain in place for five years, after which it must be removed or replaced.

11.   A half hour is the average amount of time a couple spends making love. There's not a whole lot of long and languid lovemaking going on, except for the first few months to year of a couple's life together. We're all just too darn worried about wasting time! When will we learn that efficiency isn't always best? Perhaps the reason that most women fake orgasm is that most men fake foreplay.

12.   The clitoris has twice as many nerve endings as the head of the penis (8,000 vs. 4,000). It may not seem possible that the tiny clitoris packs an even more pleasurable punch than the head of the penis, but it's true.

13.   Read on to learn the truth about pregnancy and ejaculation, oral herpes and HPV.

Pregnancy and ejaculation: Millions of sperm can swim their way to your eggs in pre-ejaculatory semen (the semen that leaks out of the penis when the male is aroused). This is more than enough to get a woman pregnant.

Oral herpes: More than twenty years ago, doctors discovered that herpes simplex (in the mouth) could be transferred to the genital area and infect the recipient with the disease.

HPV: Human Papilloma Virus is so common that some scientists believe that 80 percent of all sexually active men and women have been exposed to it. Some people get genital warts from it, some do not. HPV is even associated with an increased risk of developing cervical cancer, so it's smart to get screened for HPV the next time you have your annual pap smear.

14.   Heterosexual men say they'd like to have their partner initiate sex more of the time. Men want to be wanted. Women need to learn to take some responsibility for making sex happen—and what better way than to do the seducing once in a while? Chances are, your mate will be thrilled!

15.   Missionary Position # 2 provides the most clitoral stimulation. Sexual positions that put the pubic bones of both partners in close contact are most likely to create clitoral stimulation. The clitoris, after all, is stimulated by direct touch—by the penis tugging on the lips of the vagina and by pressure. Making love facing each other with legs extended basically makes all of the above possible.

16.   After five years, cohabiting, unmarried couples statistically have more sex than their married counterparts. The commitment of marriage is great for love, but not so great for sexual frequency. Cohabiting couples are likely to be the least committed of all the cou-

ples mentioned. Why? A cohabiting couple is usually still deciding about the future of the relationship. Sure, some cohabitors are together for life, but for most commitment is uncertain. Perhaps it's this uncertainly that keeps cohabitants auditioning for the future. The more emotionally comfortable a couple is (i.e., married folks), the more sex seems to become optional.

17.   Between 10 and 20 percent of people admit to cheating. Surprising, huh? With all of the talk about infidelity (not to mention the headlines about some very public figures) you might have been expecting a 75 percent cheat rate. But most random samples suggest that, nationwide, infidelity numbers are relatively low. (The exception: In big cities like New York, Los Angeles and San Francisco, cheating rates are higher.)

How Neurotic Are You About Your Body?

How you feel about your body has a lot to do with whom you choose to date and how you act inside of a relationship. Therefore, it's important to know if you are being neurotic about your body—and if the way you feel about yourself is affecting some of the most important choices and actions of your life. So read on, and see if you are neurotic. (Hint: most of us are.) Then see how this might be hurting your love life.

1. When I go by a mirror, I

    a. Almost never look at myself.
    b. Look, and like what I see at least 50 percent of the time.
    c. Look, and like what I see more than 75 percent of the time.

2. I think my breasts are

    a. Too big or too small or not the right shape.
    b. Okay, but I would change them somewhat if I could.
    c. Just fine. I'm happy with my breast size and shape.

3.   I think my thighs are

   a.   Way too big or too thin.

   b.   Sort of too big or too thin.

   c.   Fine as they are; I'm pleased with the way they look.

4.   I think my butt is

   a.   Too big or the wrong shape.

   b.   Okay, but I would change it if I could.

   c.   Fine. I like the way it looks.

5.   I think my face is

   a.   Not anywhere near attractive enough.

   b.   Attractive, but I would change it if I could.

   c.   Fine. I like the way it looks and wouldn't change it in any major way.

6.   When I try new clothes on

   a.   I get depressed and angry at myself—nothing makes me look the way I'd like to.

   b.   I find enough clothes that I feel I look good in.

   c.   It's a really nice experience because I like the way clothes fit me and the way I look in them.

7.   When I take my clothes off in front of a partner

   a.   It's no fun. I prefer it when it's dark, or I'm under the covers, or at least I'm not stared at.

   b.   It's sexy—even though I'm aware of body flaws, I'm comfortable and enjoy the experience.

   c.   I feel appreciated and sexy. I love taking my clothes off in front of my partner.

8. **When I wear a swimsuit**

   a. Does not apply. I never (or almost never) wear a swimsuit in public.
   b. I don't feel I'm at my best, but I get over being self-conscious.
   c. I'm comfortable—I feel I look good.

9. **When I have sex with a partner**

   a. There are several positions or acts I won't do because of the way my body looks when I do them.
   b. There are things I do in bed that I feel unattractive doing because of the way my body looks. But I definitely don't let that stop me.
   c. I like my body in bed and I feel attractive and sexy when I am making love.

10. **I worry about my weight**

   a. At least once a day.
   b. At least once every few weeks or so.
   c. Very rarely; it hardly crosses my mind.

SCORING

Give yourself one point for each *a* response, two points for each *b* response and three points for each *c* response.

10-11 POINTS

You hate your body and it is interfering with your life. When you feel this bad about your body, it inhibits your sexuality. When a woman feels really unattractive she may not think she is worthy of anyone wonderful—and may settle for someone unworthy of her. You sound so down on yourself that you may not try to go out for dates, or if you are married, you may let yourself be treated badly. Or you may have a partner who finds you attractive and sexy but you loathe yourself so much that you don't let him get really close or wild with you in bed. You are probably convinced that you are undesirable, but no matter what you look like, there is someone out there who will want you. First, however, you need to get into a frame of mind where you feel good about yourself.

12-21 POINTS

You have your ups and downs about your body—but let's face it, you're neurotic too. You'd go after quite a bit of it with a surgical knife if it weren't so expensive or scary, and you obsess about your weight or some part of your body's inadequacy. Sure, you do have moments when you feel pretty good about yourself, and that's great. But you need more of those moments, and less doubt. It's time to work on the inner you! Read the analysis for some helpful approaches.

22-30 POINTS

You're doing great. Sure you've got some self-criticism—what woman doesn't in today's body-conscious (body-crazy) world? It is hard to love your body—even models obsess about one "flaw" or another. Still, if you can like most of it most of the time—and not let it interfere with your love life—you aren't letting body image defeat you. Congratulations!

ANALYSIS

1.   We humans are vain creatures—we love to look at ourselves. So, if you are an exception and don't like to see yourself, that says that you are suffering from some ego problems. You need a change of attitude. Otherwise, you punish yourself daily—and you don't need a psychologist to tell you that beating up on your self-image daily is a bad thing. Of course we all have off days. But we should have at least some "on" days, or it's going to affect our ability to love and accept love.

2.   We have all been done a terrible disservice by the fashion, beauty and movie business. They have sold us the idea that there are only a few sizes and shapes of breasts that are beautiful and exciting. This is really rubbish. "Perky" breasts are the breasts of women under forty, very small-breasted women, women who have not had children or women who have had plastic surgery. To make a certain, temporary breast size and shape the standard for all women is sheer madness. And most mature adult men don't buy into it. They love their partner's breasts because they are hers. It is women who obsess most about this stupid standard. Fight back—love the breasts you have!

3.   Women obsess about their thighs even more than their breasts! I'm not sure who declared a universal thigh shape—but miniskirts, narrow pants and tight jeans have decreed that women are supposed to have legs that are not so much different at the top than at the bottom! Fortunately there is a countervailing trend that wants women to be fit and strong, so leg muscle has become sexy.

But still, many of us are genetically programmed to carry weight in our thighs—and that's just the way it's going to be. Your look, whatever it is, can be sexy.

4. And then there are our butts. Men tend to like butts in a lot of different shapes and sizes. If yours isn't exactly as you would like but it doesn't continually bother you, that's acceptable. But if your feelings prevent you from wearing pants or jeans, or cause you to worry if some guy sees you from behind—or stop you from having sex "doggie style"—then a revision of attitude is way overdue.

5. Most of us like our face a bit—even if we loathe our bodies. Usually there is one feature or more that stands out—our eyes, our smile, our cheekbones. It might be a love/hate relationship (if only there wasn't that bump in my nose), but you should be able to take some real pleasure in the way you look in the mirror. If you can't, it means you are either depressed or too hard on yourself.

6. Trying clothes on is stressful for almost every woman. It's hard to look into that three-way mirror and feel divine. Sizes don't run true from manufacturer to manufacturer, and it is hard to imagine how something on the rack will look on a body. Still, it shouldn't be an ordeal. If you can never enjoy trying on clothes, you need an attitude adjustment. Take some pleasure in shopping. You don't have to look perfect to look sexy.

7. Taking clothes off in front of your partner is a real test of how good you feel about your body. Granted, not all of us are free enough spirits to do a striptease; but slowly taking clothes off of each other is a titillating part of seduction and lovemaking that shouldn't be lost because negative body image inhibits you. Too often the lack of pleasure in one's body limits sex to beginning between the sheets in a dark room rather than in sexy mutual undressing.

8. Who doesn't have swimsuit blues? Only the most perfectly proportioned of us feel great in a bathing suit. Bathing suits show any extra fat (although some have been ingeniously rigged to do some camouflage), and looking perfect is generally out of the question. Still, if you have literally given up swimming or other water sports because you won't be seen in a bathing suit, it's too much of a sacrifice. Fair enough to roll your eyes about donning a bathing suit; not wise to change your life because of it.

9. And speaking of giving up things because of body neuroses . . . some of you answered *a* and *b* on question nine, which means you think how you look is directly affecting how you experience your sex life. What a bad deal! Sex is all about losing inhibitions, giving yourself over to pleasure and experimenting with new and favorite ways to be aroused. If you are so much "in your mind" during sex because you feel awkward or embarrassed about your body, there is no way you are going to enjoy sex as much as you should. Don't let self-consciousness do this to you.

10. Okay, so we all obsess about our weight. But how often we think about it makes a difference. If you are thinking about it every day, this topic has gotten too much of your attention. Imagine how much energy you are wasting feeling bad about your body. You can change that! And not only by losing (or gaining) weight. Get active, have a body that works for you. And then make yourself concentrate on all the things you like about yourself. Let yourself be admired— and believe it.

What Are Your
Sexual Boundaries?

♥

Are you a sexually wild woman, up for anything, damn the consequences? Or do you have strict morals and little need for experimentation? Maybe you are wilder than you think you are—or not as wild as you'd hoped. Take this quiz and find out!

Respond YES or NO.

1. If an attractive man who was not your date was seated across the table from you and touched your toes with his—might you let him continue?

2. If it was an attractive woman—might you let her continue?

3. If a guy you were dating told you about an explicit fantasy he had, would you tell him an equally explicit one of yours (if you had one)?

4. If you were single, and the guy was at least 20, would you have a sexual relationship with him if he was 10 years (or more) younger than you?

5. Would you flirt seriously with a darling delivery person?

6. Would you have an affair with a married man if you thought no one would ever know?

7. Would you ever go to bed with two men at the same time?

8. Would you consider being in a non-monogamous relationship?

9. Would you take your clothes off at a wild beach party where everyone else was doing the same thing?

10. Would you wear a "see-through" dress with nothing under it but panties?

11. Would you make love in an airplane bathroom—knowing that there might be a line of people waiting when you both came out?

12. Would you make love at night on a public beach—knowing that some people might come along and see you?

SCORING

Give yourself one well-deserved point for each YES.

0 POINTS

You have pretty conventional boundaries. You are not going to take any chances with exhibitionism or unorthodox sexual relationships. You are like most people—still, just for fun, you might want to reconsider flirting with that delivery guy.

1 – 3 POINTS

Every now and then you feel mischievous. For example, you had that wild night at a party in 1992 . . . but in general, you stick closely to the tried and true. You have fun and take few risks.

4 – 8 POINTS

You are a wild thing (or a wild thing wanna-be)—and proud of it! You like breaking boundaries and may have stored up several fabulous stories for your old age. In fact you probably have lived through some incredibly awkward situations; still, you probably haven't taken on the really big taboos that often lead to explosive consequences.

9 – 12 POINTS

Need a lawyer? You're a high-flying lady and a born rule breaker! You know that the rules weren't meant for you, and even if they were, you know you can handle anything. Still, remember that some of your wilder adventures haven't turned out so well, and you might consider that the next time someone offers you a wild night in bed, especially if his name is the Marquis de Sade . . .

How Much Sex
Do You Need?

♥

We all talk about how much sex we'd love to have if we weren't so busy, so tired, so distracted. But let's be honest: Maybe we're not having wild-and-crazy soap-opera-quality sex because, well, we're just not that interested. To find out how much between-the-sheets action you really crave, answer the following questions.

1. **Given the choice, you would rather**

   a. Turn off the alarm and sleep as late into the morning as decency permits, and then a bit longer.
   b. Have the man in your life roll over at 6 A.M., nibble on your neck and go full throttle into your favorite brand of wake-up call.

2. **You would rather**

   a. Spend an entire evening cuddling and kissing.
   b. Spend 45 minutes in the most sweat-inducing sex of your life.

3. **You would rather**

   a. Sneak in an afternoon romp in a king-size bed, giving new meaning to the words "full-service hotel."
   b. Spend an entire day at the crème de la crème of spas, indulging in every treatment known to woman, from toes to tresses.

4. **You would rather**

   a. Spend the afternoon shopping for—and scoring—the perfect pair of shoes, with your best girlfriend in tow.
   b. Spend the afternoon in bed with your favorite guy, searching for and finding the ever-elusive G-spot.

5. **You would rather**

   a. Spend a rainy evening curled up on the sofa with a truly gripping novel and an afghan pulled up to your chin, a cup of steaming tea in hand.
   b. Hit the sack early for some pre–prime-time nooky.

6. **You would rather**

   a. Enjoy a raucous evening with the girls, ogling male strippers and downing potent potables with cutesy umbrella garnishes.
   b. Enjoy a raucous evening with your mate, doing your own striptease—followed of course, by steamy sex.

7. **You would rather**

   a. Experience one solid day of complete peace and quiet: no kids, no friends, no partner.
   b. Experience one solid day of lovemaking with your partner: no kids, no friends, no phone.

8. You would rather

    a.   Delve into a long, intense and loving discussion with your partner about your shared future goals, plans, hopes and dreams.

    b.   Be scooped up and carried over the threshold of your boudoir for a steamy session of lovemaking.

SCORING

Give yourself one point for each *a* response.

0–1 POINTS

You're a sex machine! Your partner must be some hunka-hunka burning love. You'd rather have sex with him than spend the day at a fabulous spa like the Golden Door? We say: "You go, girl!"

2–3 POINTS

You're sexually satiated. Once in a while, something, somewhere, will tempt you away from a booty call. But most of the time, sex with your favorite guy is first on your list.

4–5 POINTS

Chances are, you're slightly undernourished in the sex department. Rethink your hectic schedule to find some well-deserved time for the pleasures in life (including intimacy with the one you love).

6–7 POINTS

You're a no-nooky woman. Since your sex drive is hovering around the "I'd rather grout the tub" level of enthusiasm, you need to give your relationship another look. Yes, alone time can be blissful, but be warned: If you've lost all interest in passionate sex (or any sex at all), you may be losing interest in your guy, or vice versa. Then again, it's possible there is a physical explanation. If you're worried about your lack of sexual interest, a visit to a professional sex therapist might be a good idea.

How Do Your Fantasies Rate?

It's been a long time since *My Secret Garden* was published, but those of us who read Nancy Friday's book blushed—either because of the explicitness of the fantasies or because our own fantasies were so paltry compared to the ones we read. Of course there is no reason to get competitive about fantasies . . . still, it's fun to think about what you fantasize about and what it might mean.

Respond TRUE or FALSE.

1. I still have sexual fantasies that I first thought of when I was a teenager or younger.

2. I have had fantasies about being taken against my will by a stranger.

3. I have had fantasies that include me, a man and another woman making love.

4. I have had fantasies that include me and two men making love.

5. I have had fantasies about making love with another woman, just the two of us.

6. I have had fantasies in which I am a man or have a penis.

7. I have fantasies about being a sex slave to a number of men.

8. I have fantasies that involve being tied up.

9. I have fantasies about dominating a man sexually.

10. A large number of my sexual fantasies are just about the sexual act; the lover is faceless—sometimes it's just body parts.

11. I have very romantic sexual fantasies about my partner or someone else I have been intimate with.

12. Some of my fantasies need to include degradation in order for them to be exciting.

13. I share and act my fantasies out with my partner—or I have with a past lover.

SCORING

Give yourself one point for each TRUE response.

0–3 POINTS

Fantasy Deficit
You probably block out the idea of most "edgy" fantasies because you think they are wrong or dirty. Or you are frightened that they

mean some kind of dress rehearsal, and you don't want to think you would put any of these things into action. But most people do not put their fantasies into reality—that is precisely why they're called fantasies: They allow you to go somewhere that might not be possible, desirable or pleasant in real life. It's not dangerous to give your mind a few erotic venues. Think of it as a virtual playground, not as something that needs actualization.

4–8 POINTS

A Fantasy Fan

If you have this many diverse and "naughty" fantasies, you have probably learned how to enrich your erotic core by allowing yourself to explore a wide variety of themes—settling on a number of them as erotically effective. There's not much you steer away from.

9–13 POINTS

Fearless Fantasy

This list has included a number of taboo topics, so if your score is this high, you've included a number of fantasies that most people find too fearsome to utilize. But not you! Still, I haven't included any fantasies that are dangerous or indicate any difficulties. If some of the things you think about do worry you, look at the following explanations for each fantasy.

ANALYSIS

1.   Most people find a fantasy and if it works for them, they might keep it their whole life. It's not immature or stunted in any way—it's a little like a sexual blankey, the baby blanket some people keep that makes them feel warm and secure. Sexual fantasies can be like that too.

2.   Probably the most common sexual fantasy women have is the fantasy of being sexually ravished by a stranger. It doesn't mean you really want it to happen—it is just a way of experiencing loss of sexual control without really being scared, hurt or humiliated. This theme has also been reinforced by "women's" romances—the dark, beckoning stranger who doesn't take no for an answer. In real life it would be rape and a horrific experience. But in fantasy it is all pretied up and really isn't scary. If it *is* scary, then it's not a sexual fantasy—it's fear or perhaps a flashback from a terrible encounter. If you have fantasies that scare you, talk to a counselor about them.

3.   Women have been eroticized so thoroughly in movies, advertisements and other media that even heterosexual women often are attracted to each other. However, heterosexual women usually don't feel comfortable fantasizing about a one-on-one with another woman, so they often imagine an erotic three-way (which is easier because the presence of a guy legitimizes being in this situation). This fantasy can also occur because a guy has suggested the idea with the hope of getting a woman interested in the real thing. But most do not take this fantasy to the next level. Don't worry that enjoying this in your brain is any promise to make it happen in real life.

4.   In its own way, this fantasy is just as edgy as thinking about sex with two women and a man. The fantasy is about being the center of attention, stimulated in all ways you can think of, and at the same time! Some women won't allow themselves to think of this because their morality dictates that this would make them sluts. But for the woman who just wants to imagine being as sexually alive and catered to as she could possibly be—this fantasy is a major turn-on.

5.   This is a more personal and intimate fantasy about being with another woman. If you have this fantasy you probably have more than a minor attraction to other women and you may be trying out

the fantasy to see how important that attraction is to you. It may be something you want to try in real life—or just an attraction you use to put extra-erotic zip into your heterosexual sex life.

6.   Don't worry—the vast majority of the time these fantasies have nothing to do with really wanting to be a man. They involve fascination with the power of male sexuality, the desire to own the kind of powerful, aggressive sexuality that men do and curiosity about what it would be like to experience the sexual sensations that men have. This fantasy is more common than you might think!

7.   Sexual slavery fantasies are common because they allow a woman to be sexually indulged and overtaken with pleasure without signing up for multiple partners—so she can have this pleasure without being a "bad girl." The sex slave scenario, with its themes of sexual submission, has a heavy-duty erotic charge for a lot of women. In fact, it is often intense for women who are powerful in real life and are tired of being in control. They may use this fantasy to luxuriate in powerlessness—and not have to deal with the issues that this would engender in real life.

8.   Same trip. Being tied up is a common fantasy because, again, it relieves you of being responsible for the sex acts you are about to enjoy. You are powerless to resist, so all kinds of erotic but taboo things can be done to you. Besides that, there seems to be a separate erotic charge from being restrained, perhaps because the idea of being teased and brought to the brink of absolute pleasure without being able to do anything about it means that one can be a sexual glutton without feeling the usual pressure to reciprocate.

9.   This is a much less common fantasy for women than being sexually subordinated. In this case, the charge comes from dominating a man, literally putting him underfoot and having him beg for the

slightest sexual favor—perhaps even sexually humiliating him. It may be more common among women who never get to exercise this kind of power in real life and want to live in the male role (as they imagine it) or find that exercising power and aggression is a turn-on because it is so different from the way they operate during real sexual sessions.

10. This is more often a male fantasy, but women have it too. In some people's minds it would be disloyal or wrong to make love to an actual person, but by just concentrating on disassembled body parts, no real person is visualized; hence no real act of infidelity (or actual sexual encounter) has occurred.

11. This is the classic female fantasy, but—surprise—it is also the classic male fantasy as well. One of the most common sexual fantasies is reliving great moments, mining them for additional erotic power and creating additional experiences. Not all women want romance in every one of their fantasies, but most have a storehouse of loving imagery and treasured memories that they bring out repeatedly. Of course, if you are focusing on romantic imagery of one partner while you are with another, it could be disconcerting or make you wonder who you really want. Most women, unless they are really alienated from their sexual partner, don't bring up romantic images of someone else during lovemaking; however, it is not uncommon for women to spiff up a somewhat ordinary lovemaking session by inserting a really compelling fantasy man.

12. Most women will not admit it, but a considerable number of them get an erotic charge from imagery that goes beyond sexual submission and into degradation. Sometimes these images are so violent, submissive or bizarre that the women seek help from psychologists because they are worried and want to know the origins of these strange scenarios. It's true that some of these images stem from unre-

solved childhood traumas (such as abuse or incest), but many are linked to less-troubling origins. These images are another way of giving up control—or even the rat race of having to be the person in charge. This has nothing to do with "real life." It is usually a release; once arousal is over, the fantasy loses its power.

13. It takes two confident people to share their private thoughts—much less act them out! You should never feel that fantasies have to be a rehearsal for real life. But acting out fantasies can be hot, hot, hot—and can build trust and intimacy as well. You just need to be very clear about which fantasies you both think translate well into playful reality—and deserve a place in your sexual repertoire. Maybe it's trite to say that the couple who plays together, stays together, but using fantasy mutually, and exploring thoughts never shared with anyone before, almost always makes a couple's sex life seem more special, exciting and satisfying.

Is Your Foreplay Fabulous . . . or Does It Fall Flat?

♥

Sex isn't just about intercourse. In fact, it's pretty hard to earn a degree as a world-class lover unless you spend some time studying the preliminaries—and you're even closer to excellence if you don't consider foreplay to be preliminaries! Answer these questions to find out how you stack up when it comes to the cuddling, tempting, teasing moves that lead to terrific sex.

Respond TRUE or FALSE.

When you're with your partner, you:

1. Engage in lots of passionate, unhurried kissing *before* you take off any clothes.

2. Nuzzle your partner's neck, shoulders and other above-the-belt zones for more than a few minutes before you begin to sexually stimulate each other.

3. Almost never have sex without at least 10 (but preferably 20) minutes of pre-sex passion.

4. Touch your partner's genitals in an arousing way for at least 5 (but ideally 10) minutes before having intercourse.

5. Enjoy having your own genitals stroked seductively for at least 5 to 10 minutes before having sex.

6. Receive oral sex during approximately 75 percent of your lovemaking trysts.

7. Initiate oral sex during at least 75 percent of your between-the-sheets encounters.

8. Occasionally use a vibrator (or other sex toy) to spice up foreplay.

9. Occasionally share a fantasy or read erotic passages to each other before having intercourse.

10. Occasionally watch an erotic movie together before hitting the sack.

11. Seductively undress each other or wear erotic lingerie or clothes for each other.

12. Regularly light candles, share a bubble bath, break out the massage oil or set a sexy scene before getting down to business.

SCORING

Give yourself one point for each TRUE response.

0–3 POINTS

Don't Flunk Foreplay!

All of us are capable of wild passion, but even the most passionate lovers require a bit of seduction and stimulation before intercourse can reach hollering heights. Besides, if you're not smooching, touching or fantasizing together on a fairly regular basis, your love life (not to mention emotional intimacy) is probably not all that it could be.

4–8 POINTS

You're Coming Along!

You usually try to do something sexy to set the erotic stage before you move on. But consider asking for (and doing) a little bit more. Instead of kissing for a scant 5 minutes before getting horizontal, smooch for 10, even 20 minutes at a time. The longer you linger over each other, the greater the satisfaction you'll experience.

9–12 POINTS

You're a Foreplay Phenomenon!

The simple fact that you take your time and are willing to engage in some mutual experimentation means that you're both foreplay fanatics—in a good way. Congratulations! Of course, you can always add another sexual trick to the mix, so never stop exploring, teasing or pleasuring each other.

ANALYSIS

1.   There's nothing as seductive as a good smooch. Kissing, all by itself, is a fine art and an act of love that stirs the soul as well as the body. The lips are almost as good as the eyes at melding two partners. The bottom line: Limiting your lip-locking is a foreplay no-no.

2.   Let your lips wander. Oft-neglected areas such as the back of the neck or the shoulder blades can be surprisingly sensitive when reacquainted with a lover's mouth. Deny your partner this kind of all-over pleasure and you deny him some of sex's sweetest delights.

3.   Do double time. Would you run your car for only a minute on a subzero day and then decide that it was revved and ready to take on the highway? Of course not. Humans are no different—we need plenty of juice to keep humming along smoothly. Sex without fore-play presumes instant desire and arousal (which is definitely not pos-sible for most women). Great lovers wait—and drive each other over the edge with their mouths, hands and bodies to make the experi-ence even more passionate, intimate and meaningful.

4–5.   Give—and you shall receive. You need to touch each other below the belt to make sure that you're both totally ready for inter-course. Reciprocity isn't just fair, it's sexy, and it will bring you closer together. Plus, if this kind of petting tends to be a one-way street (one of you gives but never gets), resentment—and less satisfying sex—is sure to follow.

6–7.   Overcome your qualms about oral sex. Many men and women feel that oral sex is somehow disrespectful or dirty. Others feel guilty for receiving pleasure while their partner is not. Though these fears are understandable, keep in mind that in its own way, giv-ing great oral sex can be as pleasurable as receiving it. After all, getting your partner all hot and bothered is a powerful feeling. So reassure your mate that you love to make him feel good (and that he makes you feel good too). Then reinforce your words by doing some initiating on a regular basis.

8. The truth about sex toys. Gadgets, vibrators and other sexual aids aren't substitutes for a partner, but they can enhance pleasure. For instance, vibrators can touch hard-to-reach areas (such as the G spot) and can produce incredibly intense sensations (and orgasms!). A great lover isn't threatened by accessorizing sex. After all, mutual pleasure and comfort is the ultimate goal, no?

9. Take a foray into fantasy. The brain is the ultimate sex organ. In other words, you can tease each other with your minds by reading erotic stories, swapping steamy dreams, doing some creative role playing, even dressing up. If you can act like a sultan, a sex slave or a stowaway on a pirate ship without cracking up or feeling too silly to enjoy it, you'll get a chance to explore new erotic territory, see your partner in a different light and add some spice to your love life.

10. Have a video adventure. Sure, most erotic videos aren't targeted toward women, and the whopping majority don't bother with plot, but chances are you won't be watching after the first 5 or 10 minutes anyway. So pop in a cassette, make fun of the silly dialogue and get in touch with your inner drama queen.

11. Undress for success. Undressing your partner (or undressing *for* your partner) can be an integral part of the anticipation and excitement of sex. But after the first few months, too many couples get so efficient at performing the act that they dispense with sensuous disrobing and just get naked. Don't. Unbutton each other's shirts slowly, or slip off lingerie seductively. Make the experience last—and the pleasure will last too.

12.   Make a sense-ation. Foreplay isn't just about touch. Ideally, it helps all of the senses work together to make lovemaking a more exciting experience. So try drawing an aromatic bath for your sweetie, light your favorite scented candle or slather on massage oil. Taste, inhale, smell and touch, and pleasure will follow.

Does Your Sexual Communication Help, or Hurt, Your Relationship?

♥

Talking about sex is hard, but it is essential for transcendent sexual satisfaction; it might even be necessary for everyday okay sex. Silent sex may be most common, but that means your partner has to be a mind reader. Let's see what you do and don't do and see if we can't show you the wisdom of a more verbal sexuality!

1. When you get undressed, you are

    a.   Silent and in a hurry to get under the covers.

    b.   Usually kissing and murmuring endearments.

    c.   Saying pretty hot things, like "I want you soooo bad!"

2. When he first starts to touch you, if it isn't exactly right, you

    a.   Say nothing.

b. Take his hand and put it where you want it.

c. Take his hand and say, "Could you touch me like this . . . ?"

3. If he is inside of you and it isn't quite the right angle, you

a. Say nothing—you take whatever you get.

b. Say something later about what you would like more.

c. Tell him to move a little to the right or left, or whatever works.

4. When he asks you, "Did you come?"

a. You say yes, even if you didn't.

b. Say yes, if you did. Say no if you didn't—with no further explanation.

c. Say yes if you did; if you didn't, you tell him either "No, but I'm fine and don't need an orgasm now," or "I didn't, and I really need you to help out because I need to come" (or something like that).

5. Regarding contraception,

a. You and your partner have never really talked about it.

b. He asked if you are using something and you said yes.

c. You have mutually discussed what would be best for the both of you.

6. If he is doing something you don't like or don't want to try, you

a. Suffer it silently.

b. Push his hand away or say no.

c. Stop and talk about why you are not keen on this; or discuss it sometime out of bed and come to a mutual decision.

7. **If you are having a fantasy—or want to try one during sex— you**

    a. Feel guilty, say nothing, and try to stop.

    b. Feel slightly guilty, say nothing, but go ahead and have it.

    c. Tell him you want to have this fantasy and see if you can share it together.

8. **If there is something physical—breath, weight, dress, etc.— that is turning you off, you**

    a. Say nothing, but it affects the way you feel.

    b. Tell him to get his act together (don't kiss when he has bad breath, etc.).

    c. Talk about a way you both can change unpleasant habits together (join a gym, joint diet, shopping for clothes together, etc.).

9. **When sex has been particularly good, you**

    a. Smile.

    b. Say, "That was great."

    c. Tell him what it was that made it so special; pour on the compliments.

10. **When you feel that he doesn't want you enough, you**

    a. Get quiet and distant—or angry and unavailable.

    b. Ask him if he is seeing someone else or accuse him of not finding you attractive anymore.

    c. Bring up the facts (how much less sex there is) and offer some possible explanations (depression, anxiety, being overwhelmed at work, problems in the relationship, etc.).

11.   When you want to try something new, you

a.   Are too embarrassed to mention it.

b.   Bring it up during lovemaking.

c.   Talk about it at some time other than during sex; maybe refer to its use in a book or movie.

12.   If you are having a long period of disinterest in sex, you

a.   Just turn your back or subtly indicate you are uninterested.

b.   Tell him, "It's not you," and don't talk about it further.

c.   Suggest going jointly to a therapist, or tell him you are going to go yourself.

SCORING

Give yourself zero points for each *a* response, one point for each *b* response and two points for each *c* response.

0–7 POINTS

You are probably in an unsatisfactory sexual relationship—or you and your partner are unbelievably lucky to be on the same sexual page. You don't talk nearly enough. Your score indicates that you may need to make a special effort to actually talk to each other—without enough feedback, positive or negative, your partner may not know if he is pleasing you or not.

8–13 POINTS

Some communication here—but not enough that is direct, specific and timely. You might be doing all right together, but read on for some guidance.

14–19 POINTS

You seem to be a good communicator, but ask yourself if there are many things left unsaid or unnegotiated. You probably have a good sex life—but if you are more open and directive (in a nice way), things can get even hotter!

20–24 POINTS

There's probably not much you haven't tried, talked over and shared. I'd be really surprised if you didn't feel good about your sexual relationship. Since it takes two to do this particular tango, you are both to be congratulated. Both your relationship and your sexual pleasure profit from this much feedback and conversation.

ANALYSIS

1.   It's hard to say sexy things. Long-term couples might even laugh at the thought of being seductive while getting undressed. But getting undressed is sexy. Most couples forget that and get right to business. If you can slow things down, and add a bit of heightened anticipation while undressing, a little bit of verbal communication goes a long way.

2.   Taking your partner's hand to show him what you want isn't a bad tactic, but it can be a confusing one. It might be apparent to you that when you push your partner's hands away from your breast it's because he was squeezing you too hard, but he may think it's because you don't like your breasts touched at all. No amount of repositioning of his hands is going to tell him how much pressure to use. You need to talk. You need to tell him exactly how you like it. And then tell him when he's got it right. Don't feel sorry for him and fake plea-

sure if he didn't get it right. If you give him false positive feedback he has every right to think that he's got it right, and will keep doing it the wrong way!

3.   You can sound like a traffic cop giving directions during intercourse (go left, go right, take a hard right . . .) but still, a man who wants to please you really wants to know what drives you wild and what doesn't. If he is sensitive about getting feedback from you, then sex is more about him than you—and you need to have some relationship work outside of the bedroom to get him to understand what love (or even good lovemaking) means. You should feel free to point out your erogenous zones, even if we are only talking about a fraction of an angle. You can tell him later of course, but some things are hard to describe and hard to repeat unless you get instruction right then and there!

4.   Of course many—maybe most—women lie about having an orgasm sometime in the life of the relationship. They are trying to reassure a man with a tentative approach or a fragile ego; or they are just tired of having sex and they know a true answer would have their partner hard at work trying to give them an orgasm that they have lost interest in having. But feedback about what makes you climax is really important. Even beyond showing him what works, he needs to know if you are ready to stop or if you have womanly needs that need to be taken care of. He will feel a lot better if he gives you an orgasm, *some* way—with his fingers, mouth, vibrator or some other toy. How you get there is less important than getting there when you want to.

5.   A lot of men are shy when it comes to talking about contraception, except perhaps to ask if you have it covered. But there are all kinds of contraceptive choices to discuss, and they vary according to whether or not you are in a long-term monogamous relationship,

whether you can totally trust your partner, and whether you are trying to get pregnant. Just as consent has to be mutual, so do the conditions of intercourse. One cue that you are in a caring and intimate relationship is that your partner wants to have a discussion about a contraceptive method with you and that you each feel comfortable making a joint decision on what is best for your relationship.

6.   A very common male complaint is, "I want to try . . . and my partner won't hear of it. What can I do?" Of course some of the things they want (a three-way, doing it on the roof of the house) are wishes unlikely to be granted, but others are more a matter of taste. It is not a good idea to do something you loathe, because that will create alienated sexuality. But it is also not a good idea to just say no, without any further discussion. You need to be open to conversation about anything. Remember, given that you have locked each other into a totally monogamous relationship, it's only fair to seriously consider a request—since you are the only option he has. You could discuss it in a friendly manner on a "date" or over dinner and maybe look at the act in movies or books before you make up your mind. You could even try it a little and see if it is more interesting than it originally sounded. Then, if you beg off, he at least knows you went the extra distance for him.

7.   Lots of "movies" go on in people's heads during sex that are unshared and unspoken. That wouldn't be so bad if so many people didn't either feel guilty about their own thoughts or feel jealous and upset because they wonder if their partner is thinking about someone else besides them. Much better idea: Accept how common fantasy is during lovemaking and don't feel guilty about it. An even better idea is to see how many of these fantasies you can share and really spice up your lovemaking. It is almost guaranteed that confiding fantasies and/or acting out intriguing ones will make partners feel much closer to each other. Sex, by the way, will be fantastic!

8.   Bad breath may not seem like a capital crime—but it sure can ruin sex. Enduring it will make you hate making love—or you will constantly be turning your head away—which doesn't exactly build intimacy. Criticism, however, is not communication, and if it is too harsh the other person won't listen. Too many comments on weight, for example, and your partner will be afraid to take his clothes off, much less make love. Better idea: Start a healthy lifestyle together. Talk it over, plan a sport, gym, diet, etc. and do it as a couple activity.

9.   Give positive and specific feedback. It's fine to smile and tell him it was great—nothing wrong with that. But it's also a good moment to tell him, right then, what was especially good. For example, if he took his time, tell him how it made you ecstatic; or if he tried a position you really liked, talk about it and tell him you'd like to do that again; otherwise, it may all happen just once—and wouldn't that be a shame!

10.   It is always painful to feel unwanted. But suffering in silence just makes the pain worse. Certainly, it would be understandable to feel hurt and defensive, and to suspect there is another woman, or fear you are no longer attractive to him. Here is where communication comes in. You need to structure the conversation so that you might find out something you can fix. First, you need to find out the causes for his change of feelings. For example, if he is very unhappy with his life and gets depressed, that would make him unhappy with everything, including you. When he feels better, he will probably feel better about you too. The point: Conversation will let you get at the underlying problem, not just the symptom. And if you can fix the problem, it opens the possibility of fixing your relationship and your sex life.

11.   You can't try something new if you don't bring it up. On the other hand, if you "ambush" your honey in the middle of lovemak-

ing, it might be too threatening. Sexual experiments are best introduced outside of bed in a low-pressure situation and in an environment conducive to mutual decision making. One additional thought: Sometimes there is some particular squeamishness about oral sex. In this case, fastidious personal hygiene and even some decorative pubic hair trimming might make the case.

12.   If you find that you are no longer interested in sex very much (or at all) you need to talk about it. It may be caused by depression, by hormonal changes in your body (particularly right before or during menopause) or because there is a relationship or life issue that makes sexual desire feel inappropriate. You cannot shut your partner out and expect him to just accept no sex, and no explanation, forever. Just telling him it's "not about him" won't solve anything either. If your lack of sexual interest has been going on for more than three months or so, you need to talk about it with your partner and then perhaps go alone or as a couple to see a medical doctor or therapist, or both. Talking to experts—and then talking about it with each other—may start a new understanding and regenerate your sexual feelings.

Are You Sexual Soulmates?

Getting in sync with your lover isn't as simple as crawling under the covers at the same time. Do you know if the two of you are as harmonious as you could be? Answer these ten questions to see if you and your bedmate really mesh.

Respond TRUE or FALSE.

1. You and your mate have been known to trade glances across the dinner table. The implied message: Both of you are up for some between-the-sheets action for dessert.

2. You and your partner know what your respective sexual limits are and exactly how, if ever, to test them.

3. When your partner touches you, 95 percent of the time, it feels exactly right (and vice versa).

4. You both have the orgasm thing down to a science; you know exactly how to drive each other over the edge.

5. When it comes to oral sex, you two dole out (and enjoy) the love equally.

6. Your partner's smooches were perfect from the beginning and are still pretty much flawless—even in the A.M., before you've gotten up to brush your teeth.

7. Both of you are satisfied with the amount of romance in your relationship.

8. You've shared sexual fantasies, some steamy, some a bit bizarre, that you've never discussed with anyone else.

9. When you walk into a room together, or when you see your partner walk into a room, you're always beaming inside, thinking, "This is *my* man."

10. The post-sex snuggle is as satisfying as the most passionate parts of your lovemaking.

SCORING

Give yourself one point for each TRUE response.

0–2 POINTS

Mismatched Lovers

Sorry, but right now, your sex life is definitely out of sync! If your score is this low you know you need help. It's probably as much a relationship problem as it is a sexual problem because you aren't catching each other's signals or sharing or risking much of anything.

Go see a therapist who specializes in couples therapy. You can make this a lot better.

3-6 POINTS

Slightly Out of Sync

There definitely is a spark between you, but it could burn brighter. My guess is that you're just not working on your sexual relationship as much as you could. It's definitely time to move sex to the front burner.

7-10 POINTS

You've Found Your Sexual Soulmate!

You guys are hot, hot, hot! You are communicating on all levels and that's what makes your sex life so great. You have affection, spontaneity, and communication. And you like sex! Keep up the good work.

ANALYSIS

1.   For couples who are emotionally and physically in sync, a great dinner party, a fine meal, or a beautiful sunset, is enough to turn you both on. Moreover, couples who are really on the same sexual wavelength often don't have to put these emotions into words— all they do is exchange "the look," which in itself can be a big turn-on. If you haven't exchanged the look for a long time, practice being flirtatious with each other. Try out those suggestive glances at the supermarket or your daughter's soccer game and you're likely to end up scoring big-time!

2.   Sometimes it's great to push the boundaries in bed, but your partner can't know your sexual limits (and vice versa) if neither of

you feels safe enough and sexy enough to try a few risky things. Sexual soulmates know when it's time *not* to be sexually complacent. Being adventurers together and deciding which new moves to include or discard can bring you closer than ever before.

3.   Sexual soulmates know how to touch each other. If you two don't, try these "pleasuring exercises," in which each person takes a turn giving and receiving pleasure. Start by lying down and having your partner touch you lightly, stroking you from your forehead right down to your toes. As he works his way down, he should pause and ask how his touch feels. Give him honest and immediate feedback about what you like. Then switch positions. This ought to give each of you more intelligent fingers—and heighten your pleasure quotient.

4.   This skill is very much in your reach—it just requires a bit of practice. Watch your partner very closely as he gets close to orgasm, paying attention to his breathing, facial expressions, muscle tension, the way he contorts his body, and the way he thrusts. He should do the same. Then adjust your touching, kissing, stroking, or thrusting accordingly. The good news: You can learn to be sexual soulmates, if you want to be.

5.   If oral sex isn't important to either of you, this is no big deal. But usually there's at least one person in a couple who really loves it. If that's the case, you both should give and receive the bounty equally. If you're not there yet, relearn how to give oral sex seductively and with obvious relish. And when it's your turn, let him know what feels good with seductive groans when he's hit the right spot. As long as you communicate with each other about what feels good, you're on the right track.

6.   It's essential that lovers love each other's kisses—you can't be sexual soulmates without this vital form of communication. Nothing

conveys emotion and arousal quite like a kiss, except for maybe gazing into each other's eyes. If your smooches aren't causing sparks, experiment: Kiss soft, then hard, then harder still. Kiss top lips, bottom lips, both lips. Tell each other what gets your motors running. Work on your technique. You know you've gotten it right when your partner murmurs, "Do that again!"

7.   Some people love hard-core romance: candy, poems, flowers, weekend getaways—every romantic touch is welcome and needed. Others find sentimental gestures claustrophobic. Both reactions are okay, as long as you share them. If one of you is dying for more romance, but the other couldn't care less, you'll have to compromise. One way to do this: Make a list of what you like (compliments, gifts, etc.) and how often you'd like it. Then compare lists and work on bringing your romantic efforts up to your partner's needs.

8.   Allowing a partner to accompany you sexually where you've never gone with anyone else can be an emotionally bonding experience. Sexual soulmates understand that it's normal to have even the most off-the-wall fantasies—and sometimes, to act them out. If you want to try using fantasy in your sex life, start with something safe (for example, reliving your first night together), then, if you think you will both enjoy it and can handle it, reveal a fantasy that might make you feel a bit more vulnerable. You're bound to feel closer afterward.

9.   If the way your partner moves, dresses, smiles or twirls his spaghetti doesn't ever give you a shiver of pleasure, you need to make that happen. Maybe your mate goes crazy when you wear that slinky red dress. So put it on and be flirtatious and seductive—and have him do the same. Doing nonsexual but physical things together—such as exercising or dancing or even just touching toes under the

table—can also make you feel sexually connected, even when you're in public places.

10. Never underestimate the power of "afterplay." Sexual soulmates know that the sweetest time of all is after the orgasm, when you're wrapped in each other's arms. Luckily, good cuddling skills can be learned. Find out how to please each other after sex. Do you both prefer lying quietly together? Does a soft temple or foot massage appeal to you? Whatever it is, jumping out of bed and going on with the day is not the best way to end sex. Give each other postcoital quality time and you'll complete your transition to being sexual soulmates.

Are Your Orgasms as Amazing as They Could Be?

———♥———

You can predict—to the hour—when your period will arrive. You can spot a mind-numbing migraine from the very first twinge. But are you tuned in to your body's more pleasurable cues—specifically, your OP (aka orgasm potential)? Answer these questions and find out if you're getting all you can from your between-the-sheets action.

Respond TRUE or FALSE.

1. You've tried at least five different sexual positions in your quest for the ultimate "Big O." By now, you know exactly which ones work and which ones give you a charley horse.

2. You know what Kegel exercises are—and you practice them frequently. (You're even doing them now!)

3. You're not really into the whole masturbation thing.

4. You're all about turning your boudoir into a love den when it comes to nooky time. We're talking Marvin Gaye, scented candles—the whole nine yards.

5. When your partner does that thing where he thinks he's turning you on but he's really just making you sore (and annoyed), you generally *oohh* and *ahhh* anyway. You don't want to hurt his feelings. Besides, you're grateful for the effort.

6. When having intercourse, you always try to steer your partner toward your clitoris. After all, that's the most sensitive spot.

7. You and your partner have settled into a slightly predictable sex routine: First he touches you here, then you kiss him there, then . . . well, you get the idea.

8. Toys are for kids, not lovers. You prefer a vibrator-free sex session, thank you very much. (You can live without mango-flavored lube and fuzzy love cuffs, too!)

9. You know where your G spot is—or at least where the experts say it's supposed to be. And you and your mate have clocked in many hours trying to touch it.

10. Sometimes you and your partner try touching more than one of your favorite erogenous zones at the same time (e.g., he nuzzles your ear and your breasts; you kiss his neck and stroke the small of his back).

11. You and your partner have been known to trade fantasies during lovemaking.

SCORING

1.	TRUE = 1 point	FALSE = 0 points	
2.	TRUE = 1 point	FALSE = 0 points	
3.	TRUE = 0 points	FALSE = 1 point	
4.	TRUE = 1 point	FALSE = 0 points	
5.	TRUE = 0 points	FALSE = 1 point	
6.	TRUE = 1 point	FALSE = 0 points	
7.	TRUE = 0 points	FALSE = 1 point	
8.	TRUE = 0 points	FALSE = 1 point	
9.	TRUE = 1 point	FALSE = 0 points	
10.	TRUE = 1 point	FALSE = 0 points	
11.	TRUE = 1 point	FALSE = 0 points	

0–3 POINTS

Time to get in touch with your pleasure zones. It may be tough for you to get sexual satisfaction with a partner if you aren't exactly sure how to satisfy yourself. The single most effective way to learn how to give yourself intense orgasms is to touch yourself and find your most sensitive spots. That way, you'll have complete control over what is touched, how lightly or firmly and for what length of time. Experiment. Once you learn how to make yourself climax, you'll have an easier time telling your partner what feels great. And don't discount sexual aids such as a vibrator or flavored lubes. You may find that playing around with these kinds of adult toys can produce previously unimagined pleasure.

4–8 POINTS

Your pleasure potential is excellent. You avoid most of the pitfalls, even if you don't run the gamut of pleasure aids. Your orgasms are probably plentiful and passionate. Ask yourself if there is even more you can do for sexual satisfaction.

9–11 POINTS

Passion Perfect! Orgasmic Olympian that you are, it's a wonder that you ever want to get out of bed (or wherever you choose to feel the earth move). Seriously, the secret to your orgasmic intensity is the large range of things you try, your ability to know exactly what your body wants (and your ability to communicate that to your partner) and, most of all, your need to keep being creative, no matter how long you and your partner have been together.